Political Economy and Risk in World Financial Markets

Political Economy and Risk in World Financial Markets

Tamir Agmon
Tel Aviv University

Lexington Books
D.C. Heath and Company/Lexington, Massachusetts/Toronto

Library of Congress Cataloging in Publication Data

Agmon, Tamir.
  Political economy and risk in world financial markets.

  Includes index.
  1. International finance—Political aspects.
  2. Investments, Foreign—Political aspects.   3.   Risk.
  I. Title.
  HG3881.A355   1985   332'.042   84-47550

Published simultaneously in Canada
Printed in the United States of America on acid-free paper
International Standard Book Number: 0-669-08339-9
Library of Congress Catalog Card Number: 84-47550

To Ora

Contents

Figures and Tables

Introduction

P olitics is probably the most important factor in determining the way in which most of us live. It is clearly an inseparable facet of most, if not all, financial decisions. Yet a certain segmentation exists between business decision and politics in the study of finance. Modern financial theory is based on the assumption of the perfect capital market, an assumption that practically rules out any political considerations. The ever-increasing presence of government and other political organizations in the marketplace casts a shadow over the usefulness of an approach that does not consider political factors.

This book attempts to incorporate political factors into financial decisions in an explicit way. Its focus is on the application of financial risk analysis to include political considerations. The political environment is taken as given, and the firm or the investor respond to the threats and promises of the political environment.

In writing this book I have drawn on what I have learned, directly and indirectly, from many individuals. Merton Miller, Robert Aliber, and Arthur Laffer at the University of Chicago and Charles Kindleberger and Franco Modigliani at MIT have contributed much to my understanding of economics, finance, and the somewhat elusive field of international finance. Donald Lessard at MIT, Kim Dietrich and Chap Findlay at USC, and Steven Kobrin at NYU have cooperated with me in many studies that have formed the basis to this book. Many colleagues and students in workshops, conferences, and classes have raised questions and made comments that contributed to my views on the subject. As always, none of those mentioned above bears any responsibility for the final product. This responsibility is the author's alone.

Writing a book is a time-consuming enterprise. A substantial part of this time was spent away from my wife, Ora, and my daughters Tali and Danna. I am grateful for their loving help and understanding.

Political Economy and Risk in World Financial Markets

1
Political Risk Is All Around Us

International financial markets are shaped by politics and economics: The basic laws of economics push relentlessly toward market integration and worldwide global economy, while the political process practiced by governments and other interest groups is expressed by constant jockeying for special economic privileges.

The forces of economic efficiency, which if successful will lead to the rule of the law of one price, will drive individuals and business firms toward an integrated world economy. In the rarified world of the "invisible hand" of the market, all resources will be efficiently allocated, and decisions will be made in a rational economic way. Such allocation will probably result in specialization and free trade in factors of production, goods, and services.

The constant struggle of various interest groups to better their share of wealth and power results in government intervention and in the construction of barriers to the free movement of factors of production, goods, and services. The intervention of political forces and organizations makes it necessary to replace arm's-length market transactions with a negotiation process. The "invisible hand" of the pure economic model is replaced by committees and officials who affect prices through regulations and negotiations. (The process of negotiation as a replacement to market mechanism is presented and discussed in chapter 4.)

The most important political organization is the national state. One source of its importance is its ability to issue currency, to tax, and to regulate. These three functions have a substantial effect on all economic activity and are also the main sources for political risk. The interplay between these facets of sovereignty and the basic economic forces, like the laws of demand and supply, determines much of what transpires in the financial markets of the world. Both current prices and transactions as well as the behavior of the prices in the future are influenced by political factors. Political risk stems from the uncertainty that is imbedded in the process of decision making in political organizations and the impact that current and future decisions have on economic variables.

The process that creates political risk is valid in a given domestic or international market. Political risk arises from the interrelationships and exchanges among various interest groups. World-scale political risk includes the joint impact of the policies of several governments on the key economic variables in the world's markets.

The Definition of Political Risk

Although political risk is discussed briefly in the literature of international finance, it is usually a loosely defined term, and in many cases analysis is confined to its most extreme form—expropriation.[1] The emphasis on this very limited expression of political risk is maintained both in microeconomic applications, such as a feasibility study for an investment by a U.S.-based multinational corporation in a developing country, as well as in a macro analysis, such as country risk estimates. In a recent study Agmon and Findlay (1982) have extended the limited notion of political risk to include the effects of government policies and the political process of income distribution to the domestic market in the United States. This study follows this broad interpretation of political risk and focuses on the omnipresence and nonsensational nature of political risk: In other words, political risk is all around us. In this context, the case of expropriation in a developing country is an extreme and usually unimportant expression of political risk.

Political risk is defined here as the unanticipated changes in political factors that affect the relative prices of traded factors of production, goods, and services. (The term *services* includes financial services and instruments like securities and money.) The term *political factors* is used in a broad sense to include all interactions among governments and between governments and various groups of individuals. The basic behavioral assumption is that all governments are active players in the world's markets. They act and react to other governments and to other groups according to a certain pattern of behavior. This pattern may be expressed by an explicit policy (such as a five-year plan) or an economic policy. It can also be derived implicitly from the actual policies of the government in question. For analytic as well as for exposition reasons, it is assumed here that governments act as if they have a specific set of goals or are maximizing an objective function. This assumption is critical to the discussion presented in chapter 4, which deals with a negotiation situation. It is also important in chapter 2, where the basic role of the government as a perpetrator of political risk is presented, and in chapter 6, which deals with the international debt crisis.

The objective function of the government can be expressed by a vector of concrete goals, like a 5 percent annual rate of growth in the GNP, or by a more general objective, like a low rate of inflation. In other cases the objectives of the government are expressed by vague terms like "economic independence" or "balanced growth." In most cases these objectives and the resulting policies do not coincide perfectly with the aggregate wants of the community over which the government has a jurisdiction, or with the preferences of the "representative resident." Therefore, individuals do not view the policies of the government as serving their own goals. As firms are vehicles to maximize the welfare of their shareholders (and maybe of their managers), there exists a potential conflict between the goals of the government and the corporate and investors' sector in a given economy. This potential conflict gives rise to political risk.[2]

Political Risk, Taxes, and Regulations

Governments affect relative prices by levying taxes, by transferring payments, and by regulations. Both financial assets and physical assets can be taxed. (The term *tax* is used here and in the rest of the study to include a negative tax, or a subsidy.) Physical and financial assets can be taxed by various governments in different locations. A given government can exercise its taxing power on local production, on incoming goods and services, on exports, and in some cases on assets located outside its own jurisdiction. For example, inflation is a tax on money balances regardless of the location in which they are held or the nationality of the holder of the balances.

Political risk arises from the uncertainty with regard to both the intended policy of a certain government and the ultimate tax incidence. The ultimate tax incidence may differ from the one intended by the government that levied the tax. Inflation risk, which is political in nature, affects relative prices of securities and other financial assets, such as deposits in various currencies. It also may change the relative prices of real goods like oil. (More on that in chapter 2.)

One important input in the evaluation of a risky project is the correlation or the covariance between the unanticipated changes in the value of the asset under consideration and the relevant measure of wealth. Modern finance theory emphasizes the covariance between returns on a given asset and a well-diversified portfolio that represents the total wealth of a representative investor. Moreover, the returns of any asset can be divided into components that have different degrees of covariability with the measure of wealth. Random components of the return, as volatile as they may be, are not risky. They are not deemed risky because investors can diversify and thus offset this volatility.

In the case of political risk, defined on the basis of unanticipated changes, the question is what is the nature of the correlation between (1) the changes in the return as a result of political changes and (2) the changes in the value of the total portfolio or some other aggregate measure of wealth. This is not an easy question to answer. If policies were perfectly arbitrary, or at least if the joint impact of the policies of a number of governments and other political organizations on the return of financial and real assets could be described as random, then the covariance would have been zero. In this case the risk has no economic meaning. In terms of modern finance, the risk is nonsystematic. Given a small government relative to the wealth base, that may be so. This approach is suitable when the government that generates the risk is small and when its actions are not motivated by a change in the wealth of the owners of the asset in question. For example, the actions of the government of Honduras are unlikely to be determined by changes in the wealth of U.S. residents who are the shareholders of a U.S.-based multinational corporation that has some production facility in Honduras. This, however, is not the general case. In those cases where a large country's government is involved, the covariance is generally positive.

The actions of the U.S. government with regard to the windfall-gains tax were positively correlated with the changes in the wealth of a certain group of investors in the United States. The change in the price of oil triggered the so-called windfall-gains tax. The tax itself was unanticipated and was an outcome of a political decision. The same process is evident in many instances of changes in regulations. The covariance is positive because the decisions of the government are partially determined by changes in the wealth of some classes of investors or other wealth-holders. This means that political risk cannot be diversified away. The systematic nature of the political risk requires individuals and firms to develop ways and means to deal with this pervasive and ever-increasing risk.[3]

The Management of Political Risk: Avoidance and Negotiation

Political risk is all around us, but in some cases it is not immediately obvious. As was pointed out earlier, the emphasis in the finance literature on the risk of expropriation is misplaced. In most cases, this type of political risk is diversifiable. Although local management may be sensitive to that type of risk, the shareholders are not. However, the preoccupation with risk of expropriation in corporate finance, and with the risk of nonpayment in international banking, tends to mask the real source of risk.

The real source of political risk is in the daily activities of the governments of the major countries in the world. For example, let us consider an investment project by a Japanese corporation in the United States. A case in point is the investment of a Japanese company in an assembly plant for light trucks in the United States. The cashflows of this project will be affected by decisions of the U.S. government that will be made at some time in the future: trade policies, in particular voluntary restraints or any other restraints on the importation of Japanese light trucks to the United States; regulations with regard to trade unions in foreign-owned corporations in the United States (The Japanese company would like to run a nonunion shop); taxation, including withholding tax and double-taxation treaties. Although the Japanese company or any other investor may have expectations with regard to these policies, the expectations may prove wrong. Political decisions are often unpredictable.

Once an identification of the major sources of political risk has been made, the second issue is to determine what is at stake. The ultimate effect of any risk is an unanticipated change in the wealth, which is a function of the change in the relative prices, the risk, and that part of the wealth that is exposed to the change. The relevance of political risk to economic and financial decisions is a function of the level of the risk itself times the exposed wealth.

There are two major ways of dealing with political risk: risk avoidance and risk negotiation. The first approach is common in the case of any tax: that is, an attempt to utilize existing financial instruments and legal arrangements in order to avoid a tax. These financial instruments and legal arrangements operate as tax shelters. As political risk is similar to a tax, one would expect to find political tax shelters as well. One example for a world-class political risk shelter is the external currency market. This and related subjects are discussed in chapter 3.

The second approach to political risk is to negotiate a favorable deal with the government or governments in question. In a perfect market where the only considerations are those of economic efficiency there is no need for negotiations. All prices are determined in the market in an auction process, and all transactions are done at arm's-length. This elegant paradigm fails once the intermingling of political and economic factors is admitted. In many instances "market-clearing" prices do not exist, and the only way to arrive at a price is for the parties involved to negotiate. The negotiations may include nonprice considerations and side payments. Negotiations are to be expected where markets are weak. One specific case where negotiations are the rule is foreign direct investment in developing countries. This is a situation in which two organizations that possess a monopolistic power—the government of the host country and the multinational corporation—are trying to agree on investment. In addition, the market in which the proposed investment project is located is not fully developed. The result is a process of negotiation. This process is presented and discussed in chapter 4.

The two major approaches to political risk are not mutually exclusive. In some cases management can employ the two methods of dealing with political risk as two components of one procedure. The procedure of capital budgeting is a case in point.

The first step in the management of political risk in capital budgeting is the identification of potential sources for political risk. Once this is done, the project may be redesigned in order to avoid the risk. If the political risk cannot be avoided—and in some cases, such as import substitution, the investment is built on political factors—then the next step is negotiation. The issue of the integration of political risk into capital budgeting is presented and discussed in chapter 5.

By its very nature political risk involves governments and business firms. The demarcation lines are not always clear. In some cases government and business are adversaries; in other cases a given government may cooperate, explicitly or implicitly, with some business firms "against" another government. What is known as the international debt crisis provides an example of such a case.

The international debt crisis is characterized by two main dynamic processes of negotiation. The first is between the borrowers, a group of nearly industrialized countries (NIC), and the major commercial banks in the world. The second negotiating process is between the borrowing countries and the industrialized countries. The banks are not unaware of the second process, a purely political one. Indeed, they base their lending policy on the expected outcome of the political negotiation between the North and the South. This mixture of international banking and politics, which may be quite explosive and is very risky, is described and analyzed in chapter 6.

Notes

1. For a thorough but traditional analysis of the role of political risk in international finance see Shapiro (1982).

2. A general analysis of political risk from the point of view of a political scientist is presented in Kobrin (1982).

3. Cornell (1975) has developed a similar argument with regard to the covariance of changes in the monetary policy of a given country, changes in the rate of inflation, and changes in the wealth of a representative investor in that country.

References

Agmon, T., and M.C. Findlay. 1982. "Domestic Political Risk and Stock Valuation." *Financial Analyst's Journal* (November/December):74–77.

Cornell, W.B. 1978. "Monetary Policy, Inflation Forecasting and the Term Structure of Interest Rates." *Journal of Finance* (March):117–127.

Kobrin, S.J. 1982. *Managing Political Risk Assessment: Strategic Response to Political Change* (Berkeley: University of California Press).

Shapiro, A.C. 1982. *Multinational Financial Management* (Boston: Allyn & Bacon).

2
Governments as Perpetrators of Political Risk in the World Markets

olitical risk was defined in chapter 1 as the unanticipated changes in the relative prices of factors of production, goods, and services caused by the actions and reactions of governments and other political groups within and between countries. These unanticipated changes can result from direct or indirect actions by political actors. They can be related to international struggle among national states or to the internal positioning of power groups within a certain country. This chapter focuses on two ways by which political risk is expressed in the financial markets of the world. The first was triggered by the radical change in the relative price of oil. This process began in 1973 and is a major component in overall risk in the world's markets. This expression of political risk can be assigned to a process of income distribution among countries. More concretely, the change in the relative price of oil was a device by which resources were transferred from one group of countries to another. The risk element in this process has to do with uncertainty about the time pattern and the net amounts of this international transfer. The second deals with inflation. Here the main goal is to transfer resources from one group to another within a national economy. Traditional public finance and monetary economics views this transfer as one that goes from the private sector to the government. However, becasue the world of today is fairly integrated, internal transfers by means of inflation in one country are affected and have an effect on other countries as well. Therefore, inflation has an effect on the overall level of political risk in the world's market. This is particularly true with regard to the inflation in the United States, which is the subject of the second part of this chapter.

These international and national transfers of resources are risky because of the unpredictability of the final results. Many times a process of transfer is initiated by a given group in a certain country, or by a given country in the world, with a certain purpose in mind. The ultimate result is usually different than the planned or expected result. Often it is unpredictable, and the path from the original triggering event to the final outcome is rather crooked and involves many changes. This process is schematically described in a formal model in the last section of this chapter. The model highlights the inherent unpredictability, and hence the riskiness, of the political process of actions and reactions.

Political Risk as an Outcome of Planned Changes in Relative Prices: The Case of Oil Prices

One major expression of political risk in the world market is the change in the relative price of oil since 1973. The relative price of oil is one of the major variables in the world markets for goods for securities and for money. Therefore, an increase in the riskiness of oil, measured by the unanticipated changes in its relative price, brings about an increase in the level of risk in the world markets. For example, changes in the exchange rates among the internationally traded currencies are partially and jointly explained by the relative inflation among the currencies in question, by the relative changes in the trade balances, and by capital movements. All these factors are affected by a change in the relative price of oil.

The price of oil is not determined in a perfect market by economic factors alone. Both the supply of oil and the demand for oil are affected substantially by political factors, in particular by issues pertaining to transfer of resources and distribution of power among countries.

Since 1973 the supply of oil to the world market has been dominated by OPEC, which operates as an effective cartel. However, the decisions of OPEC cannot be explained solely on the basis of value-maximizing behavior of a cartel. The price leader, and therefore the leading member of OPEC, is Saudi Arabia: The decision maker is the Saudi government, and its decisions are affected by both economic and political considerations. The Saudi government has a strong interest in a stable world system and is particularly sensitive to what it regards as the danger of radical changes in the Persian Gulf region. If the Saudi government is faced by two possible price policies, it will prefer the one that will foster political stability even if the other policy has higher economic value to the cartel as a whole.[1] In order to accomplish its political goals, the Saudi government is willing to forgo economic benefits by cutting back its own oil production and by side payments to other members of the cartel. Unfortunately, there is no way to calculate in advance the effect of such political considerations on the resulting quantities produced by OPEC and through that on the price of oil. The process of political negotiations among the members of OPEC contributes to a more uncertain pattern of relative prices and therefore to a higher level of risk.

Prices are determined by the joint effects of changes in supply and in demand. Decisions with regard to the demand for oil are also taken within a political as well as an economic context. One of the major determinants in the demand for oil, relative to the demand for other forms of energy, is the issue of dependence. The question of how dependent on imported oil a country should be for its energy needs is at least as much a political as an economic issue. Given the current and expected structure of its international relations, a certain country may decide to convert a substantial part of its energy-generating facilities from oil to coal even if the coal is likely to be more expensive in a net present-value sense. That is so because this country wishes to strengthen its relations with the suppliers of coal or feels that reliance on OPEC and other net oil exporters may hamper its freedom of political action in the future. This policy is even more apparent when the alternative source of energy is present within the country itself. South Africa is a prominent example of this policy, but some Western European countries and even the United States follow this route with regard to coal and synthetic fuel. Perceptions of the political cost of reliance on imported oil do change over time and even more across politicians. Thus priorities and "national agendas" change in an unpredictable manner that in turn tends to increase the unanticipated changes in the demand for oil. Uncertain changes in the demand for oil, together with uncertain changes in the supply of oil due to political reasons, make the behavior of oil prices in the world's market riskier than it would be in a world without political considerations.

Inflation as a Source for Political Risk in the Financial Markets

Inflation is a tax on money balances and on nominal contracts that are held by wage earners and by wage payers, borrowers and lenders, and sellers and buyers of many goods and services. Therefore, the tax base of inflation is usually broad and covers most if not all facets of economic activity.

Because inflation is a tax on money balances and on nominal contracts, it is specified in terms of a given currency. Most of the analysis in this chapter is presented in terms of the U.S. dollar, but inflation occurs in all currencies. Moreover, the inflation rate and the distribution of future rates of inflation in any given currency are not independent of the current and future rates of inflation in other currencies. This interdependence is of particular importance among the major internationally traded currencies in the world—the U.S. dollar, the German mark, and the Japanese yen.[2]

The relationship among the rates of inflation over time is an outcome of the phenomenon of currency substitution. In a perfectly integrated market all currencies become perfect substitutes, or they do not exist as currencies. An example of perfect substitution is between the dollars issued by the different branches of the Federal Reserve System. Barriers to trade in money introduced by various governments make the national currencies less than perfect substitutes. The existence of supranational money markets—the external currency markets—makes the internationally traded currencies better substitutes than the rest of the pack.[3] As was pointed out earlier, the ever-changing balance of power between the forces of integration and the forces of segmentation is the basic generator of uncertainty in the world's financial markets. Yet there exists an overall sympathetic movement of the rates of inflation across currencies and over time. These sympathetic movements are demonstrated in table 2–1.

Although inflation is a worldwide phenomenon, the rest of the analysis to be presented here focuses on the U.S. dollar inflation: (1) The U.S. dollar is the central, some say the only, international currency; (2) moreover, the U.S. dollar inflation has the most effect on the world rate of inflation.

Inflation as a tax has two distinct characteristics: (1) It is not fully tractable like legislated taxes, nor is its incidence voluntary like government borrowing; (2) it is the only tax where tax avoidance and tax evasion are legal. These two characteristics contribute to both the uncertainty and the political nature of inflation. Together they make inflation—and, more precisely, uncertain inflation—one of the most important expressions of political risk in the financial markets of the world.

Inflation should be viewed as accommodating rather than as an autono-

Table 2–1
Industrial Countries' Average Annual Inflation Rates
(percent per annum)

	1952–67	1967–72	1972–79	1980–82
United States	1.5	4.6	9.1	9.9
Canada	1.7	3.9	9.0	11.1
Japan	4.3	5.9	10.6	5.2
Australia	2.5	4.3	11.9	10.7
New Zealand	3.2	6.6	13.0	16.4
Austria	3.1	4.3	6.7	6.1
Belgium	1.9	4.0	8.4	7.8
Denmark	3.9	6.1	10.7	11.1
France	3.7	4.7	10.2	12.5
Germany	1.9	3.5	5.1	5.5
Italy	3.1	3.9	15.4	18.5
Netherlands	3.0	6.0	7.6	6.4
Norway	3.3	6.1	8.6	11.8
Sweden	3.5	5.1	9.3	11.2
Switzerland	2.1	4.3	5.0	5.4
United Kingdom	2.8	6.6	15.0	12.6
Range encompassing 80% of observations	1.7–3.7	3.6–6.1	7.6–13.0	5.5–12.6

Source: *International Financial Statistics.*

mous process. *Autonomous,* or *independent, process* is defined here as a premeditated process that is designed to accomplish a certain goal. In international trade, all current account transactions like imports and exports are regarded as autonomous or independent transactions. An accommodating process is a process that makes the autonomous process possible. Traditionally, short-term financial transactions in international trade are looked on as accommodating transactions: They make trade flow easier. Inflation accommodates the transfer of resources from the private to the public sector. In this, inflation is similar to other accommodating measures like income and consumption taxes and public borrowing. Once the inflationary process is set into motion, it develops a life of its own. The dynamics of inflation can be described and analyzed by two related phenomena: the actions and reactions of rent-seeking groups and the process of inflation avoidance. The two rather similar activities make the future rate of inflation dependent on the relative political power of different groups in the economy.

The concept of rent-seeking groups was introduced by Krueger (1974). The idea is appealing in its simplicity and in its immediate applicability to a variety of instances when politics and economics interact. Whenever a government restricts the otherwise market-oriented economic activity, there is a potential rent. The existence of a rent or even a potential rent initiates action by rent-seeking groups. These groups may be organized or ad hoc. They may act as groups or as loosely organized individuals. Rent seeking is an additional cost for the society in general.[4] The cost is even higher when the mere activity of rent-seeking groups contributes to a higher level of uncertainty in the economy under consideration. To see how this happens, imagine that a certain level of initial inflation is coupled with either partial price controls or some price stickiness. In this case, a rent-seeking group will try to include the prices of its purchases in the controlled group and to free the prices of the goods and services that it sells to move at a higher rate than the average rate of inflation. To the extent that one rent-seeking group is successful in creating favorable (to itself) wealth changes or avoiding unfavorable wealth changes, it triggers a response by other groups. This is so because any favorable change in the relative wealth of one group is an unfavorable change in the share of other groups. Due to the tendency to imitate successful wealth-enhancing tactics, the unfavored groups will adopt the tactics of the favored groups. The constant struggle among various rent-seeking groups and individuals creates a constant process of unpredictable changes in relative prices. A higher volatility in relative prices means higher risk. This risk is political in a narrow and in a broad sense. It is a political risk because it emanates from the power of the government to create rents via inflation. It is a political risk also in a broader sense because it is the outcome of a continuous attempt by various groups in the society to better their share using political power as well as economic means.[5]

All this jockeying is done through changes in the rate of inflation. Empirically, these changes have been associated with a relatively high rate of inflation, although high volatility of the rate of inflation in a given currency is not necessarily related to a high mean rate.

The risk described above cannot be diversified away because it relates to a central agency in the economy: the government. Moreover, the initial decision to inflate—or to put in less blatant terms, to monetized nominal obligations—is not done independently of the general economic situation. Indeed, many studies found strong and negative relationship between the rate of inflation and the prices on the New York Stock Exchange.[6] It follows that in terms of modern financial theory, politically based inflation risk is systematic. Systematic risk does count, and so does political risk of the kind described above.

The political risk, which is the outcome of the activities of the various rent-seeking groups, is expressed in various ways. One concrete way is by driving interest rates up. Indeed, the high level of inflation adjusted interest rates in the United States in the 1980s may be related to an increase in the level of the political risk.

The relationship between the nominal interest rate, the real, or inflation-adjusted, interest rate, and the rate of inflation is given by the well-known Fisher equation.[7] The Fisher equation, named after the famous U.S. financial economist Irving Fisher, states that both borrowers and lenders will act in such a way that the purchasing power will be maintained in financial transactions. This logical statement is often presented in mathematical form as

$$(1 + i) = (1 + r)(1 + \dot{p})$$

where i = the nominal, observed, interest rate expressed in annual percentage terms;

r = the real interest rate expressed in the same way; and

$\dot{p}$ = the rate of inflation in the economy also expressed in annual terms.

Given the relevant data for the United States for the first quarter of 1984 and using the expected rate of inflation for $\dot{p}$, r the real interest rate can be estimated. For the first quarter of 1984 the numbers are (approximately)

$$(1.11) = (1 + r)(1.05)$$

$$r = \frac{1.11}{1.05} - 1$$

$$r = 5.7\%$$

This is a very high inflation-adjusted, or real, rate of interest by historical standards. Given the expected real rate of growth of the economy, it seems to be too high if *r* is taken as a *risk-free* rate. In most studies and current business analyses *r,* the real rate of interest, is considered to be a riskless rate.[8] This, however, is not the case. The real, inflation-adjusted interest rate is not free of political risk, even if it is free of default risk. Political risk is expressed by uncertainty about the future rate of inflation. The actual rate of inflation is an outcome of the political, as well as the economic, process. Indeed, the deviation of the actual rate of inflation from the expected rate of inflation is affected most by the political activity of the various rent-seeking groups. A simple numerical example demonstrates this process.

In the March 5, 1984, issue of *Fortune,* a leading inflation forecasting group in the United States was quoted to say that the rate of inflation for the next twelve month period is expected to be 5 percent; however, it may be as low as 2 percent or as high as 8 percent. Assume for simplicity that everybody agrees that the probability distribution of the actual rate of inflation for the period March 1984 to February 1985 can be presented as follows:

Actual Rate of Inflation	*Probability*
2%	½
8%	½

Given this distribution as the true and homogenous expectation with regard to actual inflation, two things are clear. First, *r,* the real, inflation-adjusted, rate of interest, should be interpreted as the *expected* real rate of interest. The actual real rate, the real cost of funds, will deviate from the expected rate. In this simplistic example, the real cost of funds will be either substantially higher or substantially lower than the expected real rate of interest. If the inflation rate at the end of the period turns out to be low (that is, 2 percent), the actual, inflation-adjusted cost of funds will be slightly more than 8.8 percent. If, on the other hand, the actual rate of inflation is high (that is, 8 percent) the real cost of funds will be 2.77 percent. The risk lies in the fact that neither borrower nor lender know on February 1984 what the rate of inflation is going to be. The actual rate of inflation and, more important, the uncertainty about the actual rate of inflation over a given period are affected by the political process both directly and indirectly. The actual rate of inflation is affected by the future decision of the monetary authorities. The monetary authorities are uncertain about the direction they should take. But even in the case in which this type of uncertainty is removed by a pre-announced and adhered-to policy, the final result is still uncertain. This indirect effect rises from the inability of the decision makers to fully understand and to respond to in a timely and correct fashion the very complex process by which the rate of inflation is determined. For example, any decision by the monetary authorities that favors a given group—for example net holders of nominal contracts in terms of U.S. dollars—will prompt other groups to respond. These groups, which are now worse off, will try, by lobbying or any other means, to restore their former status or even to improve it. This everlasting chain of actions and reactions by various groups in the economy makes uncertainty unavoidable. Moreover, the more pronounced the attempts to change the relative status of some groups, either by action or by reaction, the higher the uncertainty. It follows, therefore, that the uncertainty is positively correlated with current and future political changes both in the United States and in the industrialized world at large. A similar relationship between uncertain inflation and financial risk can be shown in other parts of the capital markets. It should be emphasized here that what makes the expected real, inflation-adjusted, rate of interest higher is the uncertainty about the future rate of inflation and not a higher expected rate of inflation. Thus, if the values of the distribution of the actual rates of inflation in the numerical example presented above would be 4 and 6 percent rather than 2 and 8 percent, the expected rates of inflation will not change but the expected rate of interest will decline. The uncertainty around a given expected rate of inflation is affected by the political process described above. Therefore, the resulting risk is a political risk.

A Model of Risk Generated by the Actions and Reactions of Governments and Other Rent-Seeking Groups

Much of the discussion presented in the two preceding sections focuses on the way by which one political actor acts and responds to the actions of other political actors. Political actors may be rent-seeking groups within an economy or rent-seeking governments in the international community. Unpredictable changes in relative prices are the outcome of this political positioning and repositioning. In the first section the triggering rested with a direct change in the relative prices of a major commodity—oil. In the second section political risk was attributed to the uncertainty about the expected value of inflation. This section discusses a general model of political risk. The model is presented in two steps: (1) The interrelationships between a direct change in the relative prices of a tradable commodity and a premeditated change in the rate of inflation are examined; (2) the same model then is extended to include a general action/reaction function and its relation to unpredictable changes in relative prices (in this case, changes in the real exchange rates).

To demonstrate the interrelationship between willful changes in relative prices, as those affected by OPEC in 1973 and possible reactions by the United States, a stylized paradigm of two countries and two periods is employed.[9] Assume two countries, A and B. A is an oil exporter, and B is an oil importer. A is producing only oil (denoted X), and B is producing only consumer goods (denoted Y). Assume one currency, issued by the government of B. In accordance with the classical free-trade model presented by Mundell (1968: 8–15), the basic system is described as follows. Domestic expenditure in A in terms of X (oil) is

$$D_a = X_a + PY_a - T \qquad (2.1)$$

Domestic expenditure in B in terms of Y (consumer goods) is

$$D_b = \frac{Xb}{P} + Y_b + \frac{T}{P} \qquad (2.2)$$

In these equations, P represents the terms of trade (price of Y in terms of X), and T represents capital export (lending) of A in terms of X. The demand for consumer goods in the oil exporting country (A) is

$$Y_a = Y_a(D_a, P) \qquad (2.3)$$

The demand for oil in the oil importing country (B) is

$$X_b = X_b(D_b 1/P) \qquad (2.4)$$

The balance of payments is given by the ex-ante relationship

$$T = I_b(D_b, 1/P) - PI_a(D_a, P) \qquad (2.5)$$

where I_a and I_b are the import functions of A and B.

Given normal conditions for stability, a transfer has a two-phase effect:[10] The first phase is the actual transfer, and the second phase is the change in the terms of trade. Such a change is required to restore equilibrium following the actual transfer.

Given imperfect competition, both on the demand side and the supply side, the classic result may change by willful action. Let us start on the supply (of oil) side. Country A, the oil exporter, is trying to affect a transfer of real resources by increasing the relative price of oil. P will go up, and domestic expenditure in A and B will adjust. Now we add currency to the system. Due to limitations of absorptive capacity and portfolio considerations, the oil-exporting country is buying short-term deposits denominated in B's currency. In this case, Country B is exporting capital to Country A. In the paradigm employed here, these are one-period deposits. In other words, Country A lends money to Country B. The deposits are denominated in nominal terms, giving Country B some discretion with regard to the deposits' value in terms of the consumer goods (Y) and allowing the government of B to affect its price level in terms of its own currency.

This process is described schematically in figure 2–1. The real price of oil, $P(Y/X)$, is depicted on the vertical axis, b_2; the price level in terms of b in period 2 is depicted on the horizontal axis. In the figure, P_1 is the initial price of oil (in relative terms). $E(b_2')$ is the expected price level in terms of b at the initial state. The oil-exporting country (A) is trying to affect a real transfer by increasing the real relative price of oil, using monopolistic power, to P_2, the initial transfer line. A possible solution is for Country B to accept the transfer, in which case K is a possible equilibrium point. The transfer would then be carried out both by an increase in P and a decrease in b_2. A decrease in b_2 for nominal deposits that were negotiated given $E(b'_2)$ would be equivalent to an increase in the real return on A's deposits. Thus, there would be a current and a future transfer.

The government of B has, however, a monopoly position in the currency market. A possible solution for B is to inflate at a rate higher than the one that is consistent with $E(b'_2)$. As long as the rate of inflation is higher than the rate that was expected at the time of the negotiation, the relative price of oil as well as the real return on the deposits would go down. This possible solution is depicted at point L. Neither K nor L are general equilibrium solutions. The final solution along the line KL would be a matter of political and economic explicit or implicit negotiations.

This stylized model is far from describing reality. It excludes many other factors that affect the final determination of the relative price of oil and uses only two actors and two periods. Despite its abstract level the model provides us with some information. The data presented in table 2–2—on the actual relationship between the changes in the relative price of oil and the changes in the U.S. price level over the period 1973 to 1981—bear out the basic relationship developed in the model.

The model presented in the first part of this section is a special case of the general phenomenon by which political risk is created by the constant positioning of various political actors. The preliminary model is extended to include more than two countries, and the specific instruments of transfer of resources specified above are replaced by a more general policy variable.[11]

Assume a world of n countries. The general policy variable is the quantity of money (defined in an agreed on way), and policy is affected by changing the rate of growth of money supply. Assume further that one of the n countries is a large country. The optimal rate of growth in money supply worldwide is determined by the rate of growth in money supply in the large country. (This assumption is consistent with the role of the United States and the U.S. dollar in today's world.)

The rate of growth in money supply in the large country is denoted as

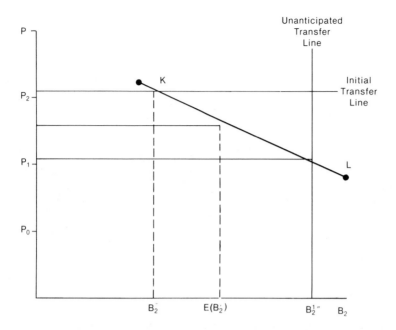

Figure 2–1. The Real Price of Oil and the Price Level

M_ℓ. This policy should be followed by the rest of the countries in the world. Thus a dynamic equilibrium implies that

$$M_\ell = M_j; i = 1, 2, 3, \ldots, n - 1 \qquad (2.6)$$

As was shown earlier, unpredicted changes in the money supply will have a real effect by changing real relative prices in the capital market and elsewhere. By deviating from the equilibrium rate of growth in money supply, some governments (excluding the large country) attempt to change relative prices in a desirable way. In terms of the generalized model, this deviation is denoted as

$$M_\ell \neq M_j \quad j = 1, 2, \ldots, n - 1 \qquad (2.7)$$

The difference between the equilibrium rate of growth in the money supply in any one of the $n - 1$ small countries and that of the large country is defined as

$$R_j = M_j - M_\ell \qquad (2.8)$$

Table 2-2
Changes in the Price of Oil and the Dollar, 1973, 1981
(percent relative to preceding period)

Year	Changes in the Price of Oil[a]	Changes in the Dollar Price Level[b]
1974	316.7	11.1
1975	(15.6)	9.1
1976	4.3	4.6
1977	5.2	6.1
1978	(1.2)	7.8
1979	28.1	12.5
1980	47.7	11.5
1981	(10.7)	9.0

Source: *International Financial Statistics.*

[a]Changes in the price of oil relative to previous year's price. Price is based on spot netback price of Saudi light crude in Rotterdam. Price is adjusted by the wholesale price index.

[b]Changes in the U.S. consumer price index.

Whenever $R_j \neq 0$, there exist forces that tend to bring the world to equilibrium by making $R_j = 0$. This is so because to sustain a disequilibrium—that is, $R_j \neq 0$ for at least one country—some countries must engage in international lending and borrowing on noncommercial basis or institute exchange controls or other forms of intervention. These policies impose costs on the rest of the world. The Bretton Woods agreement and the resulting establishment of the International Monetary Fund recognized that such costs exist and attempted to control them in an orderly manner. Thus IMF credit is usually coupled with a demand to restore balance. For the purposes of the generalized model, the adjustment process is presented as a series of changes in the exchange rates of the currencies of all the small countries in terms of the currency of the large country. The system in equilibrium can be stated as

$$B_j = (P_1, \ldots, P_{n-1}) = 0 \qquad j = 1, \ldots, n - 1 \qquad (2.9)$$

B_j is the balance of payments in country j (where j is a small country), P_j is the exchange rate of country j in terms of the currency of the large country.

When the system approaches equilibrium, equation 2.9 can be written as

$$B_j = \sum_i b_{ji}(P_i - P_i^o) \qquad (2.10)$$

using the linear terms of the Taylor expression around the equilibrium exchange rate where

P_i^o = equilibrium exchange rate in country i, $i \neq j$

b_{ji} = $\partial B_j / \partial P_i$

It is further assumed that exchange rates appreciate in proportion to balance of payments surplus according to the equation

$$\frac{dp_j}{dp_t} = \sum_i K_{ji} B_i \tag{2.11}$$

where K_{ji} describes the weight which country j assigns to the disequilibrium in country i. K_{ji} is affected by political as well as by economic considerations. In order to ensure convergence and the stability of the system it is assumed that

$$K_{ji} = \alpha_j \frac{\Delta_{ij}}{\Delta} \tag{2.12}$$

where α_j = negative constant

Δ = determinant of the B_{ji}'s

Δ_{ji} = first cofactor of Δ

Given this specification, there are $n - 1$ policy variables and the response variables K_{ji} are weighted elements of the inverse of the exchange rate matrix with α_j as weights. The change in the exchange rate of country j can be expressed as

$$P_j = \alpha_j \sum_i \frac{\Delta_{ij}}{\Delta} B_i - \alpha_{jik} \frac{\Delta_{ij}}{\Delta} B_{ik} P_k - P_k = \alpha_j P_j - P_j \tag{2.13}$$

The solution of the system described by equation 2.13 is

$$P_j = P_j^o + A e^{\alpha_j t} \tag{2.14}$$

A is a constant that depends on the initial conditions: A is positive if the disequilibrium is triggered by an undervalued currency; A if negative is the disequilibrium is triggered by an overvalued currency.

If the response function of any affected government is known, then the pattern of price changes would be known, too. In such a case there will be no risk. Technically, in the model this situation is described by a constant value for α_j. This, however, is not the case. The response of any government to the changes in the exchange rates system by other governments is uncertain. For example, if the Japanese government intervenes in the exchange market to prevent or slow down an otherwise rise in the value of the yen versus the U.S. dollar, a response by the German goverment is expected. The timing of the response and its effectiveness is uncertain. This uncertainty is expressed in the generalized model by defining α_j as a random variable drawn from some probability distribution. The probability distribution of α_j is a reflection of a host of political, economic, and social considerations. It is also the source of the uncertainty and therefore the risk in the exchange-rate system.

Given the model presented above, the distribution of the deviations of the actual exchange rate of country j from the equilibrium rate, $P_j - P_j o$, is described by the distribution of $AE^{\alpha}j^t$, which in turn depends on the distribution of α_j, which is a descriptor of the uncertainty of the political and economic processes. By assigning specific distributions to α_j and therefore to the deviations from equilibrium over time, concrete estimates of politically induced exchange risk can be derived.[12]

Concrete results require very specific and therefore limiting assumptions. The main contribution of the model is that it provides a clear and precise connection between political decision making and financial risk—in this case, exchange risk. Also it provides another insight into the importance of the process of positioning and negotiation by political actors—in this case, the governments of small countries.

Notes

1. This point is developed more fully in Sternlight (1984) and Agmon (1984).

2. The relationship among the rates of inflation in the major countries of the world was explored by McKinnon (1982, 1984).

3. This issue is developed and presented in chapter 3.

4. This result is derived by Krueger (1974).

5. For an application of the same approach to the stock market see Agmon and Findlay (1982).

6. For examples see Modigliani and Cohn (1981) and Pindyck (1983).

7. The original argument is presented and discussed in the classic work by Fisher (1930).

8. The rate of interest on short-term government bonds is considered risk free although government papers are not totally free of default risk.

9. This part of the model is reproduced from Agmon (1984: 248–51).

10. For the specific conditions and proofs, see Mundell (1968: 11–15).

11. An earlier and somewhat different version of this model is developed in Agmon and Arad (1978).

12. An empirical example based on the period of the pegged exchange-rate system is presented in Agmon and Arad (1978).

References

Agmon, T. 1984. "OPEC and International Financial Markets: Redistribution and Recycling—Comment" in *The Future of the International Monetary System,* edited by T. Agmon, R.G. Hawkins, and R.M. Levich (Lexington, Mass.: Lexington Books).

Agmon, T. and R. Arad. 1978. "Exchange Risk and the Unanticipated Change in the Exchange Rate." *Journal of Banking and Finance* (October):269–80.

Agmon, T. and M.C. Findlay. 1982. "Domestic Political Risk and Stock Valuation." *Financial Analysts' Journal* (November/December):74–77.

Fisher, I. 1930. *The Theory of Interest.* (New York: A.M. Keley).

Krueger, A. O. 1974. "The Political Economy of the Rent Seeking Society." *American Economic Review* (June):291–303.

McKinnon, R.I. 1984. "A Program for International Monetary Stability" in *The Future of the International Monetary System,* edited by T. Agmon, R.G. Hawkins, and R.M. Levich (Lexington, Mass.: Lexington Books).

———. 1982. "Currency Substitution and Instability in the World Dollar Standard." *American Economic Review* (June):320–33.

Modigliani, F., and R. Cohn. 1979. "Inflation, Rational Valuation and the Market." *Financial Analysts' Journal* (March):3–23.

Mundell, R.M. 1968. *International Economics* (New York: McMillan).

Pindyck, R.S. 1983. "Risk Inflation and the Stock Market." (Cambridge, Mass.: MIT Press, WP#1423–83).

Sternlight, D. 1984. "OPEC and International Financial Markets: Redistribution and Recycling" in *The Future of the International Monetary System* edited by T. Agmon, R.G. Hawkins, and R.M. Levich (Lexington, Mass.: Lexington Books).

3
Business Response to Political Risk: Risk Avoidance

O ne way to deal with pervasive political risk is to avoid it. Because political risk is generated by governments, the simplest way to avoid political risk is to step outside the jurisdiction of a specific government or governments in general. Political-risk avoidance is practiced on many levels. This chapter focuses discussion on the use of financial instruments and financial markets to avoid political risk.

Political risk has many faces. It expresses itself directly through regulations that prohibit or limit a certain action that will be taken by a business firm or an investor in the absence of such regulations. It also indirectly affects prices in the financial market. Uncertain inflation and exchange risks have a substantial effect on prices of almost all financial assets. Both are partially generated by political processes (see chapter 2). These risks transcend political borders, although regulations do stop where jurisdiction does. Therefore, political-risk avoidance depends on the type of political risk to be avoided. The external currency market provides a framework for avoiding the direct regulatory type of political risk. Currency substitution and the evolving financial instruments that make it practical provide a way to reduce the second, price-related political risk.

The External Currency Market: A World-Class Political-Risk Shelter

The growth and the development of the external currency market—popularly known as the Eurodollar market and the offshore market—are two of the most significant developments in world financial markets of the last twenty-five years. From a small almost accidental beginning, the external currency market has evolved to a complete network of financial centers spanning the globe and providing much of the innovation in international banking and finance for the world.[1] Table 3–1 presents the growth of the international bank lending and the Eurocurrency lending in the period 1970 to 1980.

Table 3–1
International Bank Lending and the Size of the Eurocurrency Market, 1970–1980
(billions of U.S. dollars)

End of Year	International Bank Lending[a]	Rate of Change[b]	Gross Measure of Eurocurrency	Rate of Change[b]
1970	117.1	—	103.3	—
1971	142.7	1.22	124.5	1.20
1972	194.1	1.29	164.2	1.32
1973	289.4	1.57	264.2	1.61
1974	359.3	1.24	322.8	1.22
1975	442.4	1.23	450.7	1.40
1976	548.0	1.24	539.9	1.20
1977	698.7	1.28	663.1	1.23
1978	904.7	1.29	844.6	1.27
1979	1,110.7	1.23	1,068.6	1.26
1980	1,321.9	1.19	1,294.7	1.21

Source: Johnston (1982).
[a]External assets of all the banks in the major countries.
[b]Compare to the previous year.

The folklore associated with the development of the Eurodollar market has it that the market started as a response of the Soviet government to political risk in the 1950s. At that time the Soviet government needed to transact in U.S. dollars, but in the days of the cold war it felt that there existed a real risk in placing these funds under the jurisdiction of the U.S. government. The solution was to transact in U.S. dollars in London. By doing that, the transactions were located outside the jurisdiction of both the U.K. and the U.S. governments. The U.S. government, or its monetary authorities, has no jurisdiction over U.S. dollar transactions outside the United States. The U.K. government and the Bank of England have no jurisdiction over transactions in foreign currencies as long as the parties involved are not U.K. citizens (individuals or corporations). What began as a solution to a specific and rather marginal problem of one country has grown to become one of the main features of the capital markets of the world today. The growth of what is basically a regulation-free market in the face of ever-growing government intervention is at least somewhat surprising.

Even more surprising is that the external currency that is located mainly in member countries of the EEC has grown the most in the 1970s. This is the same period in which the EEC countries turned from free and integrated market policy into a more particular nationalistic policy of more control of the corporate sector and trade protectionism.[2] The surprising fact is not that more business firms and individual investors flock to the external currency markets of the world: The largely unanswered and seldom-asked question is why these markets are allowed to operate. The same issue can be phrased in a more traditional way by posing the following two related questions: (1) What is being "sold" by the external currency market to both business firms and individuals? (2) What is the comparative advantage of the external currency market compared to the domestic capital markets in the major countries of the world?

The external currency markets of the world supply services of financial intermediation. In doing so, they provide the same services as any other financial market, whether in New York, London, or Tokyo. The main difference is that due to their special position, and to tacit approval by the major governments of the world, they are free from government regulations and control. The absence of government control allows the external currency market to provide one explicit and two implicit special services to the business and the investment communities: lower costs on both loans and deposit (the explicit advantage) and immediate and complimentary response to liquidity needs and a reduction in political risk due to future changes in existing regulations (the implicit advantages).

The efficiency of the external currency market in providing relatively high return to depositors and low cost to borrowers is well documented.[3] It is enough to say here that the release from reserve requirements and cumbersome reporting requirements and the ability to refuse service where it is not profitable makes the external currency markets more cost efficient in providing services of financial intermediation than their domestic counterparts. What is not discussed much in this context are the two implicit advantages; these two characteristics make the external currency market a world-class political-risk shelter.

In chapter 2 it was argued that inflation may be used by a government as a vehicle to better its country's position relative to other countries. Even when this is not the case, variable and uncertain inflation is often both the by-product of the struggle among rent-seeking groups as well as the triggering of a constant continuation of such a struggle. It follows that changes in monetary policy can be initiated to serve needs other than pure economics and finance: for example, the common belief in the United States that an election year brings about relatively "easy-money" policy. (It should be noted however, that this is not always the case, which in itself gives rise to political risk.) In some other times, tight monetary policy or credit controls may be imposed in an attempt to accomplish a certain political goal. The existence of a fully developed capital market where monetary policy cannot control credit expansion or contraction allows firms and individual investors to avoid some of the risks arising from unpredicted changes in monetary policy. The mere fact that deposits and loans in a certain currency are traded in the external currency market makes this currency less susceptible to monetary policy risks. Thus this currency becomes internationally more acceptable. The ability of the external currency market to counteract changes in monetary policy that are inconsistent with the demand for a certain money by the business sector is due to the way by which credit is expanded and contracted in these markets. Credit and money are created through the multiplier. The multiplier describes the relationship between an initial deposit into (or withdrawal from) the external currency banking system and the resulted expansion (or contraction) of credit and money. The two variables that affect these relationships are the reserve requirements and leakages. Reserves are the percentages of a given deposit that are not available for relending. The leakages are those funds that are seeping out of the external currency banking system and back to domestic capital market.

For example, if the reserve requirements are zero and there are no leakages, the system can expand infinitely. If the reserve requirements are .01 percent and there are no leakages, the system can create $100 of credit for any $1 deposited.[4] The important feature of this system is that no credit will be created unless some firms or some individuals will agree to pay for the credit. The willingness to pay is a function of the rate of return on the deployed funds. It follows that credit expansion, or contraction, in the external currency market is consistent with the demand of the business sector (including firms and individual investors). Moreover, if for some reason the U.S. government and the U.S. monetary authorities choose the credit market as a vehicle to accomplish some policy goal, the existence of the external currency market will render this policy ineffective. A point in case is the credit controls imposed by the Carter administration in 1980: The imposition of the credit controls has been to a large extent unpredictable or at least not fully predictable and has served political as well as economic considerations. The response of the business sector was relatively mild because by that time the Eurodollar market was fully functioning and the expected contraction in the domestic credit market could be compensated, if need be, by a parallel expansion in the Eurodollar market. Thus, the existence of the external currency markets for the major internationally traded currencies provides a built-in political-risk shelter. The external currency market provides political-risk reduction directly by allowing firms and individual investors to transact outside the jurisdiction of the major industrialized governments. It also provides broader political-risk reduction simply by existing. As was pointed out earlier, the existence of relatively control- and regulation-free credit markets limits the ability of the governments involved to use monetary policy to achieve political and economic policy goals.

If the external currency markets act as a limiting device on the monetary policy of national states and provide political-risk reduction services, why are they allowed to operate? The answer is a combination of a number of reasons. Habit, inertia, and the political power of the financial community are possible reasons. But perhaps the most important reason is the need of all actors in the financial markets of the world to have a neutral, jurisdiction-free financial arena for settling international transfers and for accommodating changes that cannot be made efficiently in national markets. The lack of efficiency reflects the political risk to be incurred by at least some of the participants.

The role of the external currency market in accommodating political changes is expressed in table 3–1. The year in which the market really grew was 1973, the year of the major international transfer, following the radical change in the price of oil. Most of the real transfer of resources from the Western, industrialized countries to a group of nearly industrialized countries (NIC) was effected through the external currency market.[5]

The Making of an External Currency Market: Singapore as an International Financial Center

The most complete example of how a government and an external currency market interact is in the initiation, development, and growth of the external currency market in Singapore. This currency market has many dimensions. Singapore benefited from government-initiated activity and has made a substantial step in making Singapore the international service center of Southeast Asia. Its government was involved in the creation of a comparative advantage. For the growing community of Japanese, U.S., and other multinational corporations with investment and trade interest in Southeast Asia, it is a conveniently located financial center—a "close-to-the-action" extension of the external currency market. For depositors it is one more location at which they can avoid current and future government control.

The recent and well-documented growth of Singapore as an international financial center provides insight into the complex and sometimes paradoxical role of governments in the establishment and the character of external currency markets. Singapore was chosen as a case study because nowhere else has the role of the local government and at least one more government in the region been more explicit.

The role of the local Singaporan government is best expressed by the following quote from the most authoritative source on the capital market of Singapore:

> The emergence of Singapore as a financial center is the result of orderly stimulation by the government through legislative measures and administrative monitoring by the Monetary Authority of Singapore with the objective of developing Singapore into a financial center. The government has taken

steps to create the right climate for financial institutions to establish and for financial market to flourish.[6]

Although the creation of the first Asian Currency Unit (ACU), which is the basic unit in the external currency market in Singapore, is credited to the Bank of America in October 1968, the market really took off in the early 1970s. The involvement of the government can be seen in the number of banks that were licensed by the Monetary Authority of Singapore to operate in this market. These data are presented in table 3–2, which shows that the market has grown in number of financial institutions but also that since the mid-1970s it has become more varied and "deeper" with the addition of the merchant banks. By 1980 about one-third of the ACU institutions are merchant banks.

The growth of the market is reflected in the volume of transactions. Table 3–3, 3–4, and 3–5 present various dimensions of the size and the growth of the market. Tables 3–3 and 3–4 describe the growth of the net sources for funds in the Singapore external currency markets (the deposits) and the uses of these funds (the loans). The data show a very high rate of growth in the infancy years of the market but also a very stable and healthy rate of growth in the later years. Table 3–5 provides information on the size of the Singapore market relative to the global external currency market of which it is a part. The data reveal that even in a growing overall market, the Singapore external currency market has grown more than proportionally. By

Table 3–2
Number and Type of Financial Institutions Licensed to Operate in the ACU Market, 1968–80

Year	Commercial Banks	Merchant Banks	Other	Total
1968	1	—	—	1
1969	9	—	—	9
1970	14	—	—	14
1971	19	—	—	19
1972	24	1	—	25
1973	37	9	1	47
1974	44	11	1	56
1975	52	13	1	66
1976	54	13	1	68
1977	60	17	1	78
1978	64	20	1	85
1979	73	27	1	101
1980	77	30	1	108

Source: Monetary Authority of Singapore as presented by Tan (1981:131).

Table 3–3
Growth of the Deposits in the Singapore External Market, 1968–79
(millions of U.S. dollars)

Year	Deposits of Nonbanks	Rate of Growth from Previous Year
1968	17.8	—
1969	97.9	5.50
1970	243.7	2.49
1971	237.7	0.97
1972	398.7	1.68
1973	912.8	2.29
1974	1614.2	1.77
1975	2067.7	1.28
1976	1960.3	0.95
1977	2254.6	1.15
1978	3600.0	1.59
1979	5771.4	1.60

Source: Monetary Authority of Singapore.

Table 3–4
The Demand for Loans in the Singapore External Currency Market, 1968–79
(millions of U.S. dollars)

Year	Loans to Nonbanks	Rate of Growth from Previous Year
1968	1.4	—
1969	0.9	0.64
1970	13.9	15.40
1971	188.8	13.50
1972	600.9	3.18
1973	1226.1	2.04
1974	2697.7	2.20
1975	3472.5	1.29
1976	4386.6	1.26
1977	5281.2	1.20
1978	6376.8	1,21
1979	8484.0	1.33

Source: Monetary Authority of Singapore.

1983 this part of the world's external currency market accounted for more than 5 percent of the total market size.

The external currency market in Singapore is one of many locations of the world's external currency market. Some locations are very developed, like

Table 3–5
Gross Measure of the Size of the External Currency in Singapore Relative to the Global Market, 1976–83
(billions of U.S. dollars)

Year	Global Market	Singapore	Singapore as Percentage of Global Market
1976	595	17	2.86
1977	740	21	2.83
1978	949	27	2.84
1979	1232	38	3.08
1980	1524	54	3.54
1981	1861	86	4.62
1982	2057	103	5.00
1983[a]	2056	105	5.11

Source: *World Financial Markets.*
[a]June 1983.

London, which is the central location of the external currency market. Others are small and limited to interbank transactions only, like the Cayman Islands.[7] The geographical distribution of international financial centers is not well understood. Different centers can be explained by using different theories, some of them financial and some of them rooted in location theory. One way to examine the growth of a given center of the external currency market is by estimating their "factors endowment." The factors of production employed in the supply of services of international financial intermediation can be classified into the following four categories:

1. Geography-related factors of production;
2. Infrastructure-related factors of production;
3. Skill and other human capital–related factors of production; and
4. Government-related factors of production.

The first category includes physical proximity to the markets to be served: time-zone aspects (that is, the ability to communicate during working hours with other markets in their working hours, and climate and geographical location (accessibility from other central places). The second category includes communication and transportation services and commercial and residential facilities (real estate markets). The third category includes the characteristics of the labor force, like the written and spoken language and the availability and the cost of skilled labor. The fourth category has to profound effect of the stability of the market. Thus the Hong Kong market has been affected greatly by the uncertainty associated with the future political structure of the colony.

In the case of Singapore, the first three factors of production were in place. What put the icing on the cake was the premeditated actions by the Singapore government and, at least for the time being, the tacit cooperation of other governments, in particular the Japanese government.

As was pointed out earlier, the external currency market that provides political-risk avoidance services is sanctioned by governments. Singapore is a case where this is done both by commission and by omission. The Singapore government has sanctioned a formal arrangement, the ACU, whereby it waves all taxes that it can collect. This is basically an economic decision because the ACU banks would not be there without the tax haven created by the government. Yet after a period of attempting to screen between the ACU market and the local market, the government has relaxed the exchange controls and thus created a link between the two segments of the market. From a global perspective, the Singapore government is extracting a rent by "leasing spaces" in a tax-free market. This rent has two components: an income component to the Singapore economy, which provides labor and other services to the large and growing international financial community in the ACU market; and a loss component to those governments that in the absence of the external currency market in Singapore would collect taxes and other payments directly or indirectly. The growth of the Singapore market points to at least a tacit cooperation of these governments.

Singapore is to a large extent a regional international financial center. The growth of the market is associated with the growth of foreign direct investment in Southeast Asia and with the growing role of Japanese companies in this market. Table 3–6 presents data on one segment of the market.

The dominant role of the Japanese is clear. Japanese issuers also play a substantial role in the Asian bonds market, and the yen is second only to the dollar. Given the close relationship between the corporate sector in Japan and the government of Japan, it is highly likely that the active role of Japanese corporations and financial institutions in Singapore is implicitly accepted by the government. It may supply the Japanese government with a vehicle to test the implications of liberalized capital market, without paying the political price of liberalizing the domestic Tokyo market. Yet the Japanese can, to an extent, reverse the trend by not allowing Japanese corporations to participate in the external currency market in Singapore. On the other hand, the more entrenched the Japanese corporations are in the market, the easier it becomes for them to avoid such reversal.

The Singapore external currency market is a creature of political decisions including political decisions by the Singapore government to establish the market and by other governments, mainly the Japanese government, to

Table 3-6
Floating-Rate Certificate of Deposit (FRCD) Issuers by Nationality, 1977–80
(number of issues)

Year	Japanese		European		Others		Total
	No.	%	No.	%	No.	%	
1977	2	100	—	—	—	—	2
1978	13	72	2	11	3	17	18
1979	28	93	1	3	1	3	30
1980	21	78	2	7	4	15	27

Source: Monetary Authority of Singapore as presented by Tan (1981):151.

implicitly sanction its existence. It is paradoxical, but dialectically correct, that this market is a major provider of political-risk and government-control avoidance.

Currency Substitution: The Ultimate Weapon against Inflation

The issuance of currency is a necessary but not a sufficient condition to exert political seniorage. A sufficient condition is that the currency under consideration will be used. A currency, or money, is used to provide three kinds of services: These are traditionally presented in terms of the demand for money as a unit of account, the demand for money as a medium of exchange, and the demand for money as a store value. As in most other cases, the quantity demanded will change with changes in the price of money, all other things equal. If other currencies are substitutes for carrying out one or more of the functions of money, then people and corporations will switch from one currency to another. This is not so surprising as it might be within a context of a portfolio of capital assets in which a substitution is both expected and observed. For example, the recent capital inflow to the United States and to U.S. dollar-denominated capital asset is an expression of such a substitution.

The existence of political risk expressed by a substantial uncertainty about the rate of inflation affects the demand for the currency in question downward. In particular, the uncertainty about the inflation affects the demand for money as a unit of account, and the demand for money as a store of value. A secondary and less pronounced effect is on the demand for money as a medium of exchange.

Uncertainty about the future rate of inflation makes it risky to use currency as a unit of account. If an individual signs a nominal contract to perform some services and to receive payment in nominal term, the real value of the contract is uncertain. If a firm contracts to purchase some materials on an open invoice basis for ninety days, the same firm may sell its product also on an open invoice basis for 180 days. Uncertain inflation introduces a substantial element of risk to the firm. This risk is additional to the usual business risk and, as pointed out earlier, is political in its origin. Currency substitution is a possible solution. The individual and the firm denominate their contracts in a more stable currency. In some cases, they may opt for a synthetic multi-currency unit like the Special Drawing Rights (SDR) or the European Currency Unit (ECU), which are baskets of several currencies weighted by an agreed-on formula.

Currency substitution can reduce the political risk involved in using currency, or short-term deposits, as a store of value. Two possible ways of doing so depend on the institutional and legal environment. One way is to hold non-domestic and more stable currency as a store of value. In many, if not all, the countries in Latin America, where the rate of inflation is high and variable, large amounts of foreign currency, mostly U.S. dollars, are held by individuals. Another and more sophisticated way is to establish foreign-currency-linked deposits. Such arrangements are very popular in Israel and were common in Brazil. These foreign-currency-linked bank deposits are sanctioned by the government as a way to channel currency substitution in legal ways. Again, as in the case of the external currency markets, the government plays a role in providing political risk-avoidance services, which the government in its actions brought into being.

Currency substitution, as a subject for academic concern, was introduced by Miles (1978). A similar notion has been advocated in a series of studies by McKinnon (1982, 1984). These researchers, however, are following observed behavior and providing a more orderly explanation to existing behavior.

The advent of currency substitution is closely related to the change in the exchange-rate regime from the Bretton Woods type pegged exchange-rate system to the current flexible-exchange-rate system.[8] A main characteristic of a textbook version of the flexible-exchange-rate systems is that it insulates the money supply of one country from that of the rest of the world.[9] A less frequently discussed attribute of such a system is that it increases the political risk associated with uncertain inflation. (Friedman was aware of such a development, and he always argued for a preannounced and stable monetary policy that would make uncertain inflation inconsequential.) The rise in inflation worldwide since the introduction of the flexible exchange rates in 1971 and the increase in the variance of the inflation in the last twelve years is evidence supporting an increase in the level of political risk. This evidence is presented in table 3–7.

High inflation induces currency substitution. Corporations and investors tend to move away from their own currency to a more stable one. This is particularly true in countries with technically developed capital markets like Israel or Brazil. The following exploratory model focuses on borrowing decisions by corporations.[10]

For exposition purposes, a highly stylized paradigm is employed. Assume that the financial manager of a given firm operates under the following conditions. There are only two relevant periods: The firm buys the necessary factors of production in the first period; all the output resulting from the employment of the factors of production is sold during the second period, and the resulting income is distributed among the various claimants. The firm's income is a random variable denoted by Y. It is assumed that a prespecified part of the necessary expenditure for the factors of production is

Table 3–7
Mean Rates of Inflation and Standard Deviation of the Rates of Inflation for the United States, Japan, Germany, and the World, 1960–80
(annual percentage)

	United States	Japan	Germany	World[a]
First Subperiod Fixed Exchange Rates, 1960–72				
Mean	1.48	0.92	1.82	1.96
Standard deviation	1.70	1.34	1.68	1.46
Second Subperiod Flexible Exchange Rates, 1973–80				
Mean	10.78	9.98	5.58	10.71
Standard deviation	4.41	10.33	3.50	5.10

Source: *International Financial Statistics.*
[a]The world is a GNP weighted average as in McKinnon (1982).

financed by borrowing the necessary funds. Thus, the financial manager has to borrow a given proportion of the needed outlay for a prescribed duration.[11] This proportion is denoted B. The proportion B can be raised by using one or more of N debt instruments, or loans in terms of N different currencies.

Using one currency as a numeraire, each one of the N currencies' loans has different distribution of repayments in nominal terms of the numeraire currency. Even if the expected value of all loans at the end of the period is the same, the distribution will vary with the currency. Because the future spot exchange rates of all currencies in terms of the numeraire are affected by the distribution of the future rate of relative inflation, which in itself is partly determined by political considerations, it follows that the future value of the loan varies partially with the degree of political risk associated with the currency in question.

The decision problem faced by the financial manager can be specified as follows.[12] Let χ_j denote the proportion of the given borrowing raised by borrowing the jth currency where

$$\sum_{j=1}^{N} \chi_j = B \tag{3.1}$$

Then the repayment (interest and principal) in period two is

$$\sum_{j=1}^{N} \chi_j \tilde{R}_j \tag{3.2}$$

$\tilde{R}_j$ equals a variable describing the payment in terms of the numeraire. $\tilde{R}_j$ is the product of the contracted amount in non-numeraire currency times the spot exchange rate at the time of the payment. The latter is not known at the time of the borrowing.

The relationship between the operating income of the firm, Y, and the debt repayment (assume no tax) is:

$$Y - \sum_{j=1}^{N} x_j \tilde{R}_j \leq 0 \qquad (3.3)$$

If equation 3.3 is positive, then the difference is paid to the shareholders or is transferred to retained earnings. If inequality equation 3.3 is negative, there is a penalty cost. The penalty cost (PC) represents the need to raise more funds under a "distress" situation.

The financial manager is assumed to maximize the following objective function:

$$\underset{x_j}{\text{Max}}\, E - \alpha PC \qquad (3.4)$$

where

$$E = E\left(Y - \sum_{j=1}^{N} x_j \tilde{R}_j\right)$$

α = the probability that $Y - \sum_{j=1}^{N} x_j \tilde{R} < 0$ and PC occurs

αPC = the expected value of the penalty costs

The expected income minus the penalty cost, $E - \alpha PC$, is the expected monetary value. Assuming a constant penalty cost (PC) the choice of x_j, the currency of borrowing, will affect both α, the probability of a negative cashflow, and E, the expected income minus the debt repayment. Given α, the choice of the financial manager is obvious: Choose a borrowing policy such that

$$\sum_{j=1}^{N} x_j \tilde{R}_j$$

is at a minimum. In other words, choose a borrowing policy in various currencies that will minimize the debt repayment bill in terms of the numeraire.

However, α, the risk measure, is not independent of the currency choice, expressed in the model by vector of x_j. Consequently, the decision should be optimized in terms of the expected income E, and the risk measure, α.

The concept of risk-return trade-off, known in the finance literature as the efficient frontier, was introduced to modern finance literature by Markowitz (1952). The same basic idea is employed here to derive the optimal currency mix in multiple-currency borrowing. The efficient frontier is derived by choosing a value for one variable and optimizing the other. This procedure is repeated for all values of the first variable. In this case, the probability of a negative cashflow, α, is parameterized, and the optimal value for E is computed. The model is stated as follows:[13]

$$\text{Max } E\, Y - \sum_{j=1}^{n} x_j \tilde{R}_j \tag{3.5}$$

$$\text{s.t. } Pr\left(Y - \sum_{j=1}^{N} x_j \tilde{R}_j < 0 \right) \alpha$$

$$\sum_{j=1}^{n} x_j = B$$

$$x_j \geqq 0; j = 1, 2, \ldots, N$$

Assuming that one currency is the numeraire, then we have one nominally fixed repayment scheme and $N - 1$ "foreign" (or non-numeraire) currencies with variable payments schemes. The actual payment is linked to the future spot-exchange rate between the foreign exchange and the domestic currency.

Assume that $j = N$ is the numeraire currency. The difference between repayment schemes in numeraire and non-numeraire currencies is defined as

$$R_j^1 = R_j - R_n; j = 1, 2, \ldots, N - 1$$

An interesting comparison is between a numeraire currency borrowing and a multicurrency approach. Thus let us define

$$Y^1 = Y - BR_n$$

as the cashflow minus domestic currency debt service (repayment). The maximization problem then becomes

$$\text{Max } E = E \sum_{J-1}^{N-1} x_j R_j^1$$

$$\text{s.t. } Pr\left(Y - \sum_{j=1}^{N-1} x_j R_j^1 < 0 \right) = \alpha \tag{3.6}$$

$$\sum_{j=1}^{N-1} x_j = B$$

$$x_j = 0; j = 1, 2, \ldots, N-1$$

Following Agmon, Ofer, and Tamir (1981), it can be shown that given a multivariate normal distribution for the variables $(Y^1, R_1, \ldots, R_{n-1})$ and restricting α to be equal or less than one half, an efficient frontier in the plane (E, α) can be derived. See figure 3–1. The efficient frontier contains two types of solutions. The first is numeraire currency only. This solution is depicted by point A where both E and α are zero. The second type of solution is multiple currency solution. This solution will be located on the segment DF in figure 3–1. Given a linear objective function $E - \alpha PC$ as was assumed in equation 3.4, an optimal solution can be obtained, as shown in figure 3–2.

Choosing a currency j as the vehicle for raising part or all of the necessary funds will affect both the expected monetary value of the corporation in question and its financial risk. The risk is a function of both the political risk associated with the currency under consideration and the relationship between the changes in the value of the currency of the borrowed funds and the cashflow generated by the company. The political risk is expressed by the unanticipated changes in the exchange rate between the currency of the borrowed funds and the numeraire. This market risk is affected upward or downward by the firm specific correlation specified above.

A Two-Currency Example

In order to discuss the major decisions involved in multiple-currency borrowing and to demonstrate how political risk can be avoided by this financial policy, a specific two-currency case is examined. Assume a U.S. firm that needs to borrow $1 (which is consistent with the proportion B in the total investment). The financial manager has identified two options:

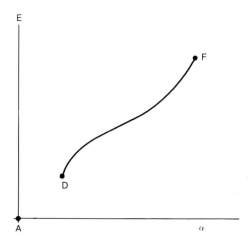

Figure 3–1. The (E, α) Efficient Frontier

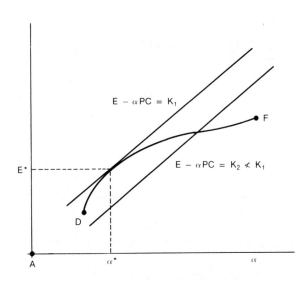

Figure 3–2. An Optimal Solution

1. A one-period term loan in U.S. dollars with 12 percent interest rate p.a.
2. A one-period term loan in DM with 8 percent interest rate p.a.

The two loans will be executed in terms of U.S. dollars. In the first case, the firm will receive $1 million at the beginning of the first period and will repay $1.12 million at the beginning of the second period. In the second case, the firm will receive $1 million at the beginning of the first period and will repay the dollar equivalent of ($1,000,000 × S_t^{DM})(1.08/S_{t+1}^{DM}), where S_t^{DM} is the spot exchange rate between dollars and marks today (marks per dollars) and S_{t+1}^{DM} is the spot exchange rate between dollars and marks at the beginning of the second period. Both repayment schemes are uncertain in real terms. As was shown in chapter 2, the real value of the straight dollar loan depends on the actual rate of inflation. The real value of the DM loan depends on the actual relative inflation in the U.S. dollar and in the mark.

Any measurement of risk requires a definition of a riskless measure. This is so because risk is a relative concept. For this example, it is assumed the nominal U.S. dollars are riskless. In this case, retaining all the earlier assumptions, the maximization problem can be stated as

$$\text{Max } E = e_0 X_1 e_1$$

$$\text{s.t. } e_0 - X_1 e_1 + Z(\alpha)\left[(' - x_1)\Omega \begin{pmatrix} 1 \\ -x_1 \end{pmatrix}^{1/2}\right] \geq 0 \tag{3.7}$$

$$0 < X_1 < 1$$

where

$$e_0 = E(Y - BR_n)$$

$$e_1 = E(R_1 - R_n)$$

$$\Omega = \begin{bmatrix} a^2 & C \\ C & b^2 \end{bmatrix}$$

R_1, R_n = debt repayments of the DM denominated and the U.S. dollar loan, respectively

a^2 = the variance of the firm's operating income, $\sigma^0(Y)$

b^2 = the variance of the DM denominated debt repayment

$$b^2 = \sigma^0(S_{t+1}^{DM})$$

c = the covariance between the operating income and the future spot exchange rate

The solution for the problem is a function of e, the expected interest differential in U.S. dollar terms as well as the variance of the future spot exchange rate, and c, the covariance term. The first two terms reflect the political risk, among other factors. The covariance term reflects the vulnerability of the cashflows of the firm in question to the political risk. By borrowing in more than one currency the corporation can reduce the effect of an adverse change in the future spot exchange rate, while taking advantage of the interest rates differential.

The different optimal solutions provided in table 3–8 can be translated into actual policies by assuming numerical values for the variables. In a recent study, the standard deviation of the changes in the spot exchange rate between the DM and the U.S. dollar was calculated at 14.2 percent. Using this point estimate and parameterizing c, the following results are derived.

1. If the covariance is negative or zero, the corporation will borrow only U.S. dollars.
2. If $B = \frac{1}{2}$ (debt/equity ratio of one) and if $C = .071$ the corporation will borrow only DM ($x_1 = B$).
3. If $C > .071$, the corporation will borrow both U.S. dollars and marks.

Obviously, the actual numerical results depend on the specific assumptions. It is reasonable to assume, however, that in many cases multiple-currency borrowing can be employed to reduce politically based currency and inflation risk.

Table 3–8
Multiple Currency Borrowing as a Function of c and b^2

The Value of c and b^2	*Optimal Proportion of DM borrowing (X_1)*
$c = 0$	$X_1 = 0$
$c < 0$ and $B^2 < B$	$X_1 = \dfrac{c}{b^2}$
$c > 0$ and $b^2 B$	$X_1 = B$

Notes

1. The external currency markets is the subject of many books. For a recent and thorough analysis see Johnston (1982).
2. This development is documented by Robinson (1983).
3. Johnston (1982) provides a discussion and an estimate of the market's efficiency. See in particular chapters 4, 5, and 6.
4. For a complete description of the way by which the multiplier works see Johnston (1982).
5. For a further analysis of this point see chapter 6 below.
6. Tan (1981):8. Tan provides the best and most detailed analysis of the capital markets and the financial institutions of Singapore.
7. In a recent report *World Financial Markets* accounts for centers. The centers span the world. See *World Financial Markets,* January 1984.
8. Miles (1978) is presenting a framework where the likelihood of a demand-generated currency substitution depends on the type of exchange-rate system in operation.
9. The most well-known proponent of this view is Milton Friedman (1953).
10. This section is based in part on Agmon (1982).
11. This is a rather limiting assumption. Obviously the proportion borrowed is not independent from the use of the funds and from market conditions. The assumption is employed here to focus the analysis on the currency substitution aspect of the general problem.
12. This model is based on a similar approach developed by Agmon, Ofer, and Tamir (1981).
13. This solution is different than the standard mean-variance efficient frontier. The difference stems from the inequality in the constraints. For an explanation see the appendix in Agmon, Ofer, and Tamir (1981).

References

Agmon, T. 1982. "Borrowing Decisions in a Multiple Currency World," IBEAR Working Paper, University of Southern California, Los Angeles, CA.

Agmon, T., A.R. Ofer, and A. Tamir. 1981. "Variable Rate Debt Instrument and Corporate Debt Policy." *Journal of Finance* (March):425–37.

Friedman, M. 1953. "The Case for Flexible Exchange Rates." *Essays in Positive Economics.* (Chicago: University of Chicago Press).

Johnston, R.B. 1982. *The Economics of the Euro-Market* (New York: St. Martin's Press).

Markowitz, H.M. 1952. "Portfolio Selection." *Journal of Finance* (March):77–91.

McKinnon, R.M. 1982. "Currency Substitution and Instability in the World Dollar Standard." *American Economic Review* (June):320–333.

McKinnon, R.M. 1984. "A Program for International Monetary Stability." in *The Future of the International Monetary System,* edited by T. Agmon, R.G. Hawkins and R.M. Levich (Lexington, Mass.: Lexington Books).

Miles, M.A. 1978. "Currency Substitution, Flexible Exchange Rates and Monetary Independence." *American Economic Review* (June):428–436.

Morgan Guarantee Bank-*World Financial Markets* (January) 1984.

Robinson, John. 1983. *Multinationals and Political Control.* (New York: St. Martin's Press).

Tan, C.H. 1981. *Financial Institutions in Singapore* (Singapore: Singapore University Press).

4
Business Response to Political Risk: Risk Negotiation

I n a world of perfect markets and rational behavior all prices would be determined by arm's-length transactions among anonymous actors; there would be no need for negotiation. As was demonstrated in the preceding chapters, however, the financial markets of the world are far from the rarified paradigm of perfect markets. Moreover, some if not all of the markets' participants have political as well as economic goals. Many participants, government agencies, and business firms enjoy a certain degree of monopoly power. The combination of monopoly power and political (or social) goals makes it necessary to negotiate prices and other conditions for transactions. This chapter discusses a number of such cases. Political considerations have substantial influence on the form and the outcomes of many negotiations. The most obvious class of cases is where the government is a party to the negotiations. Given the role of the government in most economies, this situation is quite common. The need for negotiation increases according to the strength of the monopoly position enjoyed by the parties to the contemplated transaction. Governments in developing countries have a very strong hold over their own markets. This strong position is expressed by laws and regulations, as well as by the economic functions that government's agencies and companies perform in those countries. Large corporations, particularly multinational corporations from large industrialized countries, do hold some degree of monopoly power as well. The juxtaposition of the different and sometime opposing objective functions and the political and economic power of both governments and corporations created a situation of political risk. This type of political risk is different than the political risk discussed in chapter 3. In the case of the political risk in the money market the risk is impersonal. In other words, each economic actor is "playing" against the system, the system being his own government or any government. In the cases to be discussed in this chapter, political risk is very specific, almost a personal matter between two teams of negotiators. In addition, risk negotiation deals with a dynamic situation. A successful attempt by a corporation to avoid or otherwise mitigate a risky situation may cause a reaction by the government. Chapter 2 presented a general model of actions and responses. However, in this case the response of one government was triggered by the policies of another government. Corporate risk negotiation is concerned with cases where the government responds to the specific actions of a given corporation.

One way to negotiate a situation of potential political risk is to shield the transaction from the reach of a government. This is particularly so where the company under consideration holds some specific advantage that it wishes to protect from the reach of a government that has political power over the company. Intratrade industry is shown to be a way to establish a political-risk shelter. The emergence of the multinational corporation has contributed to the politicization of the international marketplace. The existence of large bureaucratic organizations on the two sides of the line that separates business from government does contribute to nonmarket solutions. By the same token it contributes to a higher level of political risk.

Negotiated solutions are not general, and they depend on a specific set of conditions. Yet it is possible to outline the main features of a negotiated solution for investment decision by a multinational corporation in a developing country.

Intra-Industry Trade as a Substitute for Arm's-Length Market Prices and Transactions

The phenomenon known as intra-industry trade—that is, international trade within the same industry—does not square off with the classic paradigm of perfect and rational markets. Yet it is on the increase. Indeed, this is only one aspect of a tendency to internalize transactions within firms. It is shown below that intra-industry trade is politically motivated. In other words, it is the result of a set of government policies. Therefore the continuation of a intra-industry trade depends on the continuation of these policies. These policies may cease to be operative due to a change in government or a change in policy or both. Corporations make investment decisions and commit funds assuming that current policy will continue. These investment projects are risky: The funds are at risk.

Two popular government policies that give rise to intra-industry trade are granting a monopoly position in the local market and changing relative prices by intervention in the markets for factors of production. The two measures are commonly employed by governments in the industrialized and the developing countries.

Intra-industry trade can be regarded as a part of the process of international investment in a world of imperfect competition. Suppose that a firm is facing oligopolistic competition in the country in which the firm is domiciled and a free competition in the world market. The firm then is facing two markets that are represented by two different demand functions. The demand function in the country of domicile is downward sloping, and the demand function in the world's market is horizontal. This simple case is depicted in figure 4–1.

In the market where the government gives the firm an oligopolistic position, the firm will act as a monopolist. *DD* is the demand function of the country of domicile; *DW* is the demand function for the products of the firm in the world's market. *MR* and *MC* are the marginal revenue associated with the sales in the protected (oligopolistic) market and the marginal cost, respectively. Total production of the firm is given by the quantity *OB*. This quantity is allocated to the local, protected market and to the market of the world. The prices are *PD* and *PW* in the two markets. Where there are a number of countries pursuing this policy, creating an oligopolistic position for domiciled firms, intra-industry trade will result. Intra-industry trade—export and import within the same industry—is always a result of some imperfection in the market. In this simple example the imperfection is expressed by the oligo-

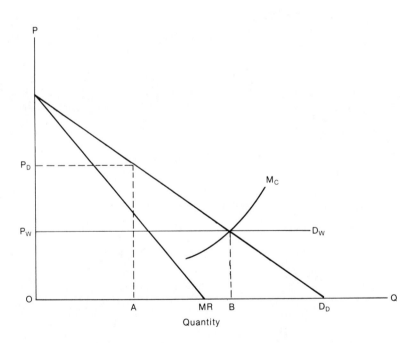

Figure 4–1. Demand in the Domestic and World Markets

polistic position of different firms in different markets. Trade becomes a vehicle to maximize rents. In some cases the monopolistic position is dependent on exporting, even when the export price is below the marginal cost of the firm. In this class of cases, common in many countries, the oligopolistic position in the domestic market is given conditionally on a certain level of export. For the firm this policy can be consistent with profit maximization if the rent in the oligopolistic market is sufficient to compensate for the losses in the exports.

This situation is shown graphically in figure 4–2. The firm is selling the quantity *OA* at the price *PD* in the protected market. It realizes a rent represented by the area *PD, PC, F, E* (the shaded area in figure 4–2). The firm is losing money in the world's market. For every unit sold at a price *PW* the loss is *PC, PW*. The firm will be willing to sell in the world market a quantity up to *AB* before giving up its monopolistic position. This is so because at this quantity the loss from the export markets is exactly equal to the rent in the domestic market. The quantity of goods to be exported under this arrange-

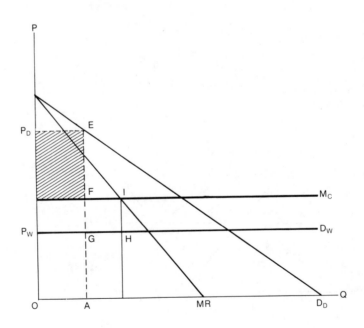

Figure 4–2. Demand Conditions with Government Intervention

ment is subject to negotiation. The process of negotiation starts before the investment that should create the export, and it continues all along. Export of that type often falls under the definition of intra-industry trade. It is political in nature and is the result of a continuous process of negotiation between the firm and the government. Because the rent of the company depends on the ability and the will of the government to maintain its oligopolistic position, there is an element of political risk in the arrangement. The risk stems from the uncertainty of both the will and the ability of the government to stand up to the original arrangement. For example, pressure by consumer groups may force the government to remove or reduce the duty and other taxes that make an oligopolistic position possible. Once the investment is in place, the cost of dismantling is fairly high. This realization may tempt the government to renege on early understandings with the company. All these factors present problems that cannot be solved by market mechanisms and prices alone. A solution requires a process of negotiation like the one described in the model below.

The policy described above, as well as the response of the firm, is a special case of what is known as an outward-looking policy. The term *outward-looking policy* was coined by Keesing (1967). Keesing defines this type of policy as "The direct transition from a simple, open trade policy to vigorous promotion of manufactured export by all internationally tolerable means." The meanning of such a policy, which is not limited to developing countries, is that the government actively intervenes in the markets for goods, services, and factors of production. The goal of an outward-looking policy is to change relative prices in order to create a comparative advantage where none exists before. The vehicle by which this goal is accomplished is investment decisions by corporations. By changing the relative prices faced by the decision maker within firms the government may be able to direct investment to desirable fields of economic activity. The desirability is a function of the goals of the government. Two common and acceptable means of affecting relative prices are (1) price discrimination between the domestic and the external markets and (2) capital subsidies. These two means as well as the policy itself introduces an additional element of risk to the investment decision of the firm.

Investment decisions are intertemporal, and capital is at least partly non-shiftable. The firm has to base its investment decisions on the relative prices in future periods. If managers or owners know that the government is trying to affect the relative prices in the economy, they have to include this information in their investment decisions. For example, if the government is following an outward-looking policy such as industrialization, resources may be directed at industrial production for export. Given the current relative prices, this type of investment is not attractive.

Making investment decisions under uncertainty is the essence of the process of capital budgeting. What makes this case different is the source and the nature of the risk. The source of the risk is the government. The nature of the risk depends on the answer to the following two questions: (1) Does the government really mean what it states? (2) Can it deliver? These two questions are at least partly political and require political as much as economic analysis.

Foreign Direct Investment and the Exposure of the Multinational Corporation to Political Risk

The search for an explanation for the existence and the growth of the multinational corporation (MNC) has occupied the center stage of research in international business. Starting with Hymer (1960), Kindleberger (1969), and Caves (1971) and continuing with Hirsch (1976) and Dunning (1973), all the explanations center around market imperfections. The imperfections may be in markets for goods and for factors of productions because foreign direct investment by MNC will not take place in a world of perfect markets. Most of the literature focuses on imperfections that give rise to oligopolistic competition (e.g., Caves 1971) or to firm specific factors of production (e.g., Hirsch 1976). The political motivation and the political risk associated with the first instance were discussed above in the first section of this chapter. Another type of market imperfection is barriers to international capital mobility. As was shown by Agmon and Hirsch (1979), these barriers create advantages for multinational corporations over domestic companies. While pursuing its own business objectives, the MNC is exposing itself to political risk. It also solves the problem by negotiating the barriers that were imposed by the government. The barriers are bypassed by replacing market transactions with internal transfers within the MNC. The MNC may be looked on as a business organization that is capable of dealing effectively with restrictions on the free movement of goods and factors of production imposed by various governments. This ability stems from the multinational character of the MNC. The MNC can internalize the benefits of efficient allocation of resources and goods in a world market while at the same time responding to signals emitted by governments in the markets in which it operates. The same ability makes the MNC more vulnerable to political risk. The MNC is exposed to political risk for two main reasons. First, because of its comparative advantage, the MNC tends to operate in countries and in fields of operation where barriers exist, so by definition the likelihood of getting involved with government and government agencies is greater. Second, the success of the MNC in negotiating the restrictions and the barriers imposed by a given government triggers a response. If, for example, the MNC is fully successful in making the restrictions nonbinding, the government will impose new and more effective restrictions. The centralized nature of the MNC and its rather high profile makes it an easier target for control than an anonymous group of investors and small companies.

The situation described above may lead to a deadlock where the two adversaries, the MNC and the host government, are vying to outsmart each other. Situations of this kind can be solved by bargaining and negotiated agreement between MNCs and host governments.

A Model for Bargaining and Negotiated Agreement between a Multinational Corporation and a Host Government

Investment activity creates economic gains. In a perfect market the gains are allocated among the owners of the various factors of production, including management in an optimal way through the market mechanism. In a world of government intervention policies and oligopolistic competition, such an elegant and clear solution does not exist. The economic gains, including rents, has to be allocated among the participants in the market. The government is the creator of some of the rents and because it has power to act claims a part of the gains. (The question of what the government does with the resources that it acquires is not dealt with here.)

The process of bargaining and one possible solution are presented in a formal model below. The optimization problem in the model leads to a characterization of the type of contracts that are preferable, or at least acceptable, to both the MNC and the government. The methodology used is similar to the one developed by Leland (1978) in connection with offshore oil leases. The contracts take into account present and future actions by the MNC or by the government of the host country, in that they emphasize the political risk involved in these contracts. The risk is an outcome of the dynamics of the possible responses of the government to changes in the conditions. One specific vector of changes is the phase of the investment.

Suppose that a MNC is considering an investment project in a given country. Let the net present value of the project, V, be expressed as

$$V = V(a, s) \qquad (4.1)$$

where V is a function of the state of nature, s, and the managerial decisions, a, of the MNC.

The net present value of the project includes all the economic gains whether they are accruing to the MNC or to the government of the host country. The value of the project, measured from the point of view of the MNC, is affected by the actions, present and future, of the host government. These actions may add or reduce the value of the project that is accrued to the MNC. For example, granting monopoly power will add to the value of the project. Taxes, regulations, and direct control over the decisions of the management of the MNC will reduce the part of the value of the project accrued to the MNC. (In some cases they may affect the total value of the project as well.) Let

$$T = T(a, s) \tag{4.2}$$

be the net effect (positive or negative) of the actions by the government of the host country on the value of the project accrued to the MNC. The state of nature, s, is at least partially a decision variable, although it may contain environmental factors that affect the policy of the government. The amount of taxes collected, or subsidies granted by the government, depends also on the managerial decisions by the MNC. Thus T depends both on a and on s. The net economic value of the project to the MNC is

$$N(a, s) = V(a, s) - T(a, s) \tag{4.3}$$

where N, V, and T are expressed in terms of net present values.

The MNC is assumed to behave as if it is risk averse. This behavior is described by the maximization of the following objective function:

$$\text{Max } F = F - P(V), j = 1, \ldots, n \text{ projects} \tag{4.4}$$

where F is the economic value measured from the point of view of the representative shareholder of the MNC. This investor is assume to have a portfolio of investments and financial assets. $P(V)$ is a cost associated with the variability of the cashflows. The variability of the cashflows is a function of managerial decisions and decisions by the government of the host country. (The relationship between the decisions of the government and the cashflows of an investment project is discussed in chapter 5 below.)

Given the objective function, the MNC behaves as if it maximizes the certainty equivalent of the project under consideration, where

$$\text{Max } B = B^*$$

$$\text{s.t. } EU(N(a, s)) = B^* \tag{4.5}$$

where B^* is the certainty equivalent associated with the vector of managerial decisions, *a*, and the state of nature, *s*. *EU* is the expected utility associated with the net economic value of the project to the MNC.

The behavior of the government of the host country can be described in two different modes. The government can act as if it maximizes the total economic gains of the project, or it may be concerned with the payments to the government only. A third possible objective that is a combination of the two former approaches is focusing on that part of the cashflows that remain in the host country.

If the government of the host country acts as if it maximizes the total economic gains, its behavior can be described by the following objective function:

$$\text{Max } EW\,(\,T(a, s)\, + \,B''\,)$$

$$\text{s.t. } T(a, s)\, + \,B'' \,> 0 \text{ and } B^* > 0 \qquad (4.6)$$

where B'' is the certainty equivalent of the economic gains of the project accrued to the residents of te host country.

The objective function described above incorporates two important assumptions. The first is that *B*, the certainty equivalent of the cashflows, is the sum of B^*, the certainty equivalent of the economic gains accrued to the shareholders of the MNC, and B'', the certainty equivalent to the residents of the host country. In other words, the value of the project is allocated in a zero sum game fashion between the residents of the host country and the external shareholders of the MNC. The second assumption is that *B* depends most on *a*, the managerial decisions of the management of the MNC. Unless their decisions will produce value, there will be nothing to tax.

The solution of this problem requires specific structure for the objective function of both the MNC and the government. In general, the optimal solution calls for some risk sharing. If the government removes some of the risk *B*, the certainty equivalent of the net present value of the project will increase, and B'' may go up as well. One specific risk that can be reduced is the political risk. To see how that reduction can be accomplished, consider the following two alternatives: (1) the MNC acts as if all contracts and agreements with the government of the host country will be enforced (in other words, the possibility of a change in the current arrangements between the government and the MNC is ruled out); and (2) the MNC takes into account the possibility that the government may alter in the future agreements and even contracts under which the investment is undertaken. In the first case the question of an optimal contract is readily solvable. The solution depends on the specific form assumed for the objective function of the government.

Like in almost all cases of bimonopoly, there is no general solution. The problem becomes much less tractable when political risk is introduced in the form of the second alternative mentioned above. One way to reduce the political risk of renegading on past agreements may be found in some form of bonding. Another potential solution is in the form of linkage like in the case of cofinancing. Both the solutions require negotiation and may require intra-firm transactions and other modes of specific, nonmarket transactions.

References

Agmon, T., and S. Hirsch. 1979. "Multinational Corporations and the Developing Economics: Potential Gains in a World of Imperfect Markets and Uncertainty." *Oxford Bulletin of Economics and Statistics* (November):333–345.

Caves, R. 1971. "Industrial Corporations: The Industrial Economics of Foreign Investment." *Economica* 38 (February):27.

Dunning, J. 1973. "The Determinant of International Production." *Oxford Economics Papers* 25 (November):289–336.

Hirsch, S. 1976. "An International Trade and Investment Theory of the Firm." *Oxford Economic Papers* 28 (July):258–271.

Hymer, S. 1960. "The International Operations of National Firms: A Study of Direct Investment." Ph.D. dissertation, Massachusetts Institute of Technology, Cambridge, Mass.

Keesing, D.B. 1967. "Outward-Looking Policy and Economic Development." *Economic Journal* 306 (June):303–320.

Kindleberger, C.P. 1969. *American Business Abroad* (New Haven, Conn.: Yale University Press).

Leland, H.E. 1978. "Optimal Risk Sharing and the Leasing of Natural Resources with Application to Oil and Gas Leasing on the OCS." *Quarterly Journal of Economics* (August):413–437.

5

Political Risk and Capital Budgeting[1]

T
he discussion in the preceding chapters has focused on the definition of political risk as an integral part of the world of today and of
the response of investors and firms to this risk. The emphasis has
been on the supply of capital and in ways that suppliers of capital in the international market can deal with political risk. In this chapter the same issues is
addressed from the point of view of the demand for capital by the business
firm. The demand for capital is expressed by the process of capital budgeting.
Therefore, in this chapter the issue is how political risk, as it was defined
earlier, should be integrated into the process of the capital budgeting. This is
a normative question that deals with what should be done. It is appropriate in
this case because in most instances political risk is ignored in the process of
capital budgeting. Yet political risk is there. In most countries in the world,
including the major industrialized countries, political factors have an important effect on the variability of the cashflows of many investment projects.
These factors may or may not be reflected in the current procedures of capital
budgeting. In this chapter the political factors are defined in a measurable
way, and their effect on the cashflows of any given investment project is evaluated. In this way political risk becomes an explicit part of the procedure of
capital budgeting. Once there is an agreed on way to measure and evaluate
political risk in the context of capital budgeting, the issue as a whole is taken
"out of the closet." It ceases to be an afterthought, an addendum in some special cases and becomes an integral part of the normal procedure of capital
budgeting. This is important because a project that seems to be devoid of
political risk may be critically affected by political factors. This situation is
demonstrated in the case study presented at the end of this chapter.

The Political Dependence of the Cashflows

Organizations, including business firms, are comprised of sets of interdepen-
dent parts, which are dependent in turn on larger external environments.

Business firms interact with the external environment where they dispose of their goods and services, output interactions. They also interact with the environment where they acquire information and materials necessary to the production process. Resource dependence both with regard to input and output is measured by the degree of control that other individuals, organizations, and government agencies have over the flows of inputs and outputs to and from the firm. Because the value of a given investment project is a function of input and output prices, control over output, input, and prices pertaining to a given project affect the present value of the project. The external environment that has control over the firm is comprised of individuals, social groups, and political organizations. In many countries the latter group is the most powerful. The effectiveness of the environmental constraints is a function of the need of the organization for external resources (how critical they are), and the extent to which these resources are control by political organizations. The greater the importance of a certain input or output to the present value of a project, the more vulnerable it is to political risk. The greater the degree of control that a certain political group exercises over this critical output or input, the greater the political risk. Given the thorough involvement of the government and other political agencies in most countries, political dependence, and therefore political risk, is potentially relevant to almost any investment project. Political dependence stems from three major sources:

1. Direct government participation in the economy;
2. Indirect control by administrative means; and
3. Income distribution through transfer payments (taxes and subsidies).

Although the three sources are not independent of each other, it is useful to discuss them separately.

Direct government participation expressed itself through the purchases and sales of government departments and state-owned companies. Many firms as well as specific investment projects do depend on sales to the government or on purchases from the government. For example, a pharmaceutical company may depend on its sales to a national health system. An investment project that aims to develop a certain weapon system is dependent on the decision of the defense department. The profitability and the present value of an investment in a nuclear power station depends on the terms of supply of nuclear fuel to be provided by some government agency. All firms are dependent on some external organizations and individuals, and the relationships are not certain. The dependence on economic decisions (sales and purchases) by the government and other political agencies is different because these organizations are motivated by political considerations. Thus a change in policy will affect spending decisions. A change in accepted mores will change the condition under which the government conducts business. Defense-related projects are subject to the former, while projects like nuclear power are subject to the latter. If the variability of the cashflows of a certain investment project depends on sales to and purchases by the government, then the project depends on political decisions and is subject to political risk.

Indirect control includes the entire range of regulatory and administrative activity of the government. Some of the regulatory activity is aimed at macroeconomic variables like the quantity of money, taxes, and the public debt. These policies affect the economy as a whole, and therefore they have an effect on the risk and the resulting value of investment projects. More relevant as a source of political risk are regulations that reflect noneconomic goals. Environmental regulations, health and safety regulations, and other special-purpose regulations change in response to the political mood of the electorate. The risk element in the dependence of the cashflows on a certain structure of regulations is that they are subject to fast and unpredictable changes. The experience of the domestic and the international airline industry over the last twenty years is an on-site case study on the effect of changes in the regulations on the variability of the cashflows. As a change in regulations is an easy way to accommodate political and social changes, the risk factor in regulatory policy is high.

Another tool of administrative policy is intervention in the markets for goods, services, and factors of production. The most common examples are minimum wages, limitation on the level of interest rates, and price controls. International trade is particularly liable to that kind of intervention. Orderly market agreements and voluntary restraints are just two examples of administrative intervention in the international market for goods. Again, the risk is not in the policy itself but in the high likelihood of changes and in the political nature of the change.

The main vehicle for income distribution is the tax system. The term *tax* is used here to include direct and indirect taxes, social security payments, and subsidies. This type of control is more general than specific. However, there are cases where specific taxes and subsidies created a demand for investment projects or where projects were initiated as a response to a specific tax or a transfer payment. Changes in the tax system may alter completely the future cashflows of a given project. Such changes are almost always the result of political and social changes. Projects that contain elements of tax shelter are particularly vulnerable to this type of political risk.

In summary, projects and firms in which some critical outputs or inputs are subject to direct, administrative control or to the tax/subsidy effect are susceptible to political risk. This broad statement covers most if not all of the investment activity. In order to make it into an effective managerial tool the list of projects subject to political risk has to be narrowed to include only projects where the effect of political risk is nontrivial. A given project can be affected by political risk in the following ways:

1. Changing the estimates of the cashflows in such a way that the present value of the project is reduced to the point where the project is no longer viable, either relatively (versus other alternatives) or absolutely (e.g., the net present value becomes negative);
2. Increasing the uncertainty in such a way that the variance of the estimated cashflows brings about an increase in the required rate of return to the point where the expected net present value (discounted in the appropriate risk adjusted discount rate) is reduced significantly. The additional uncertainty that reflects political risk is a function of the variability as well as the complexity of the external political and social environment in which the firm is operating. Managers and owners are facing two types of uncertainties. First they are uncertain about the end result of the interactions among the various interest groups in terms of changes in policies. Second, it is not clear how these changes will affect the cashflows of a given project. For example, investors and managers in Mexico in 1984 had to estimate what kind of economic program would be the outcome of the objective economic conditions and the political realities both in Mexico and in the United States. Given any program, there will be economic, social, and political repercussions. The second step for management is to evaluate the effect of the program and its repercussions on the project under consideration.

In order to integrate considerations of political risk into the procedure of capital budgeting, a normative, operational model is needed. Such a model is presented later in this chapter. The need for a routine and workable way to integrate political risk into capital budgeting has become more acute over time because political dependency as a worldwide phenomenon is on the increase. This trend is presented and discussed in the next section.

Political Risk Increases over Time

Business firms in most countries in the world, developing and developed alike, have experience greater political dependence over time. The increase is a result of a process of politicization of economic activity. In virtually each country the economic role of the government and its various agencies has expanded. Governments have responded to pressures to take increased responsibility to the macroeconomic performance of the economy. They also responded to pressures to attend to the socioeconomic welfare of specific groups in the society. The first function is carried out by the traditional tools of economic policies. Some of these tools involve the direct participation of the government, eithr through purchases and sales by the government itself or by the economic activities of state controlled companies. The second function is carried out by tax policy and by administrative and regulatory means. In addition, as the government becomes more involved in the economy it develops an organizational taste for it. Consequently, in some cases the initiation for interventionist policy is in the political agency itself.

There are many explanations for the increased role of the government in the business sector. They range from the dislocation of the old order following World War I, the economic crises of the 1930s, the immense need for reconstruction after World War II, and the North/South negotiations in the second half of this century.

In the less developed countries and the nearly industrialized countries, the politicization of economic and business activities resulted from the imperatives of rapid development under conditions of minimal availability of managerial and technical resources. In the advanced, industrialized countries it has flowed from such factors as the increasing interdependence among countries, the increasing scale of complexity of economic activities, and concerns about the discrepancies between market performance and social objectives. In both groups of countries the result is an increase in political dependence. As was evident in the preceding chapters, the process of politicization is not abating over time. On the contrary, it is growing, and it is likely to continue to grow. Whether one accepts this development and sees it as a positive trend or whether one prefers the "invisible hand" of the perfect market is not relevant. It is in the interest of the owners, and the responsibility of the managers, to develop tools to deal with the many facets of political risk. One such managerial tool is presented and demonstrated below.

Integrating Political Risk into Capital Budgeting: An Operational Model

The potential dependence of a project on its external political environment can be divided into two components: vulnerability and cost. Vulnerability is expressed by the probability that a political event that has an effect on the project will occur. It is important to note that vulnerability is not defined in terms of joint probability (i.e., an event will occur and the effect on the project will be a lower net present value). Rather, vulnerability is defined in terms of events: Examples are local content requirements, mandated local ownership, changes in tax regimes, a change in the regulatory structure, and explicit or implicit preference on the part of the government or a state-owned enterprise to do business with a certain class of firms. Vulnerability is defined as a probability distribution. For simplicity it is assumed that the distribution can be fully described by its expected value and its variance. Thus an even can be described by these two parameters. For example, management can estimate the expected value of the imposition of import restrictions within the next two years as 60 percent. The variance around this estimate is a measure of the reliability of this estimate.

Cost is defined as the actual impact on the cashflows of a given project if a given political contingency occur. For example, the imposition of price control for a period of two years will reduce the net present value of the project under consideration by $1 million. This is a simplistic example where all the necessary information is available. Normally there is limited historical experience with political events, and translating political contingencies to net present values is problematic at best. Therefore cost is also expressed in probabilistic terms. Going back to the earlier example, the reduction in the present value should be stated as the expected value of $1 million with a standard variation of $200,000. Assuming a normal distribution, this means that with a probability of about 68 percent the reduction in the net present value of the project will be between $800,000 and $1.2 million.

Political dependence is a function of vulnerability and cost. It is assumed that vulnerability and cost are independent of each other. There is no necessary relationship between the likelihood of occurrence of a given event, a likelihood that is determined on a macro, political level, and its cost implications to a certain investment project. For example, while the government is attempting to select an effective regulatory policy to carry out some social goals, its objective is modification of behavior and not changing the viability of a specific project. The political dependence of investment projects can be analyzed with the aid of the two-by-two matrix shown in figure 5–1.

The implications along the left/right diagonal are clear. Firms will be concerned only minimally with low-vulnerability, low-cost situations. All firms should be concerned with a situation of high vulnerability and high cost. Interpretation of the two other cells is more ambigious. In general, managers will be more concerned with situations of low vulnerability and high cost than with situations with high vulnerability and low cost. The former are potentially "disaster" situations that may involve personal cost to the manager over and beyond the cost to the owners.

The distinction between vulnerability and cost is critical to the analysis. Firms and managers need not be concerned with all possible political events. Indeed, most political events, even major ones, do not have much of an impact on the cashflows of a specific project. Those events that have a nontrivial effect on the cashflows have to be weighted by their probability of taking place.

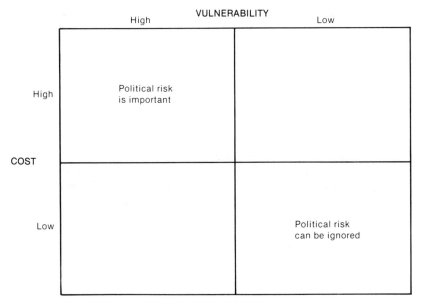

Figure 5–1. The Political Dependence Matrix

In sum, political dependence is a multiplicative function of vulnerability and cost where

$$Di = Ei^*Ci \qquad i = 1, \ldots, N \text{ political events} \qquad (5.1)$$

Ei is the probability of a given event i. Ci is the cost associated with this event. Di is a measure of the dependence with respect to a given political event. Project political dependence is the sum across all events of the cost elements pertaining to the investment project under consideration. The summation is problematic because potentially significant political events are not likely to be statistically independent of each other. Price controls and import restrictions are likely to be two parts of the same economic policy. Such relationships make the identification of a cost to an event rather difficult.

The concept presented above provides a basis for the operationalization of political dependence and therefore of political risk. Making the estimation of political risk work for the purposes of capital budgeting requires the ability to define and quantify the following:

1. The probability distributions of possible political events; and
2. The probability distributions of impacts on the present value of any given project.

An estimate of the vulnerability and the cost for any project on a period by period is also required. There are many ways to accomplish these goals. None is perfect. The method actually used will vary from one country and company to another. However, the following five steps present a concrete way to integrate political dependence into the process of capital budgeting.

Enumerate Potentially Significant Contingencies

Contingencies are defined in terms of impact on cashflows and on projects rather than environment events. Impacts are the result of resource dependencies and the potential control of future periods over inputs and outputs. Thus developing a list of possible contingencies requires an ability to identify the cricital inputs and outputs for the project under consideration, the external groups that have the ability to control or otherwise constraint the current and future flow of these critical outputs and inputs. Possible methodologies to accomplish this ability include scenario analysis, issue analysis, and actor-based analysis. Enumerating contingencies requires a thorough knowledge of the project and the political environment. The base to all analysis should be the estimate of the project's cashflows over time. The additional information is included as contingencies within the framework of the cashflows analysis.

Narrow the List to a Feasible Set of Contingencies

The list of contingencies developed in step one has to be pruned down to a workable number, maybe ten to fifteen. The criterion to choose which event to include is the potential effect on the net present value of the project. For example, only events with a potential impact of 10 percent of the net present value or more will be included in the next step in the analysis.

Estimate Vulnerability for Each Event over Time

This part of the analysis examines the probability that a given event, taken from the "short list," will occur in any time period during the duration of the project. Given that it has taken place in a given period, what are the implications for the project? For example, should it be abandoned, redesigned, or perhaps left as is?

Compute the Probability Distribution of the Costs Associated with the Events

In this step the probability distributions of the costs to the project as a function of the political events are computed. Costs should be evaluated by the management responsible for the project. The cost is expressed in terms of an expected value and a standard deviation.

Estimate Dependence as a Function of Vulnerability and Cost

In this last step the dependence function is estimated for the project as a whole. In this way political dependence is quantified as a part of the standard cashflows analysis. Sensitivity analysis can be utilized if the basic information on the likelihood of political event is scant.

The purpose of the method described above was to demonstrate that it is possible to translate the principles of political risk evaluation discussed earlier in this chapter into a practical procedure. This is further demonstrated in the case study presented in the next section.

The Chocolate Factory: A Case Study

The procedure described above has been applied to a realistic situation in the stylized case study presented below. The case study deals with an investment in a consumer good, chocolate, to emphasize that political risk is not limited to defense, communication, and other traditional areas of government activity. The risk in this case is in the home market of the company in question, but it revolves around issues of international trade.

Consolidated Foods is a large diversified food manufacturer and distributor in Israel. The company has a strong market position in many food products like edible oil, margarine, and canned fruits and vegetables. Consolidated Foods has no market share at all in the field of chocolate and sweets. This market is totally dominated by another large company, Superior Foods. Superior Foods has fifty years of experience in the production and distribution of chocolate and sweets in the Israeli market. During the last fifteen years Superior has bought, taken over, or driven out of the market all of its competitors, and it holds now a monopolistic position in the market for chocolate. This monopolistic position and the monopolistic profits attracted Consolidated Foods to this field. Moreover, the management of Consolidated feels that chocolate and sweets will fit into the existing distributing system of the company. Therefore, Consolidated Foods is considering an investment in a modern facility for the manufacturing of chocolate and sweets. The following is a description of the proposed investment project.

a. Investment in Fixed Assets (U.S. $)

Machinery and other equipment	$3,200,000
Building	2,000,000
Installation, electricity, etc.	700,000
Shipping, insurance and other costs	1,600,000
Total investment	$7,500,000

b. Cost of Production (direct cost for one tone of product ($))

Materials and wages	$2,170
Packaging	320
Energy	50
	$2,540

Capacity at full production: 6,000 to 6,500 tons of "net chocolate."

c. Sales (Forecast)

Domestic sales in full capacity: 2,600 tons of "net chocolate content" (assuming a specific composition of final product).

Domestic Prices: $9.08 per kilogram of "net chocolate."

Export sales in full capacity: 3,500 tons of "net chocolate content."

Export price: $3.00 per kilogram of "net chocolate."

Prices and quantities are based on best estimates and on the price structure of today. The most important feature is the level of production. The total duties and other payments give the domestic chocolate a 100 percent protection. In comparison, the level of protection for other food products like canned foods is 25 percent. The high level of protection is evident in the price differential between the domestic price for chocolate and the world's price. The domestic price is more than 300 percent of the world's price.

d. Pro Forma Income Statement (Full Capacity)

	(M$)	*(%)*
Sales		
Domestic	23.6	69.2
Export	10.5	30.8
Total	34.1	100.0
Cost of Goods Sold		
Materials	12.95	38.0
Packaging	4.09	12.0
Wages	1.02	3.0
Energy	0.68	2.0
Total	18.74	55.0
Operating Profits	15.36	45.0
Management Cost	1.71	5.0
Marketing	6.82	20.0
Finance	2.39	7.0
Net Profit Before Tax	4.41	13.0

The proposed investment is profitable. It has a positive net present value at a discount rate of 20 percent. The payback period is about six years. However, all the profit is derived from sales to the domestic market. The direct costs of manufacturing are $2.54 per kilogram, whereas the export price is $3.00 per kilogram. When the indirect costs (management, marketing, and finance) are added, the contribution of the export sales is negative.

Given the analysis presented above some members of the board of directors brought forward a revised investment program. According to this investment plan the capacity of the plant will be trimmed down to 3,000 tons, compared to the 6,500 tons in the original project. The required investment in fixed assets will go down to $5 million compared to $7 million. The net present value will go up, and the payback period will go down. Because the revised program does not change the assumptions about domestic sales but only removes the unprofitable element of export sales, it seems to dominate the original project.

The revised, smaller project seems to be highly desirable, but it also contain a significant level of political risk. (Other sources of risk like competitive response by Superior and technological risk are ignored here.) In this case the political risk is rooted in a single contingency: the reduction or removal of the protection on chocolate in Israel. The profitability of the project is crucially dependent on the large price differential between the world price of chocolate and the domestic price. A reduction in the tariff and other forms of protection will eliminate the profitability of the project.

The vulnerability of the project to such a contingency is affected by two additional factors. First, the trend in the world in general, and in Israel in particular, is to eliminate tariffs and discriminatory taxes. International agreements like GATT and regional agreements like those related to the EEC make this trend stronger. In addition, the good in question is a consumer good without any strategic characteristics or other externalities that single it out for protection. The current high rate of protection is based on past relationships between Superior and the government, as well as on a weak "import substitution" argument. The entry of Consolidated Foods to this market may start a price war that will be instrumental in reducing the high level of protection.

Once the high level of the protection is reduced, it is unlikely that it will be reinstated. In other words, the political contingency, if and when it occurs, will have a lasting effect on the project.

The question is now what can management do about this situation. There are two necessary steps. The first is to evaluate the probability over time of a reduction in the level of protection. The estimate of this event should be based on an analysis of past history, current policy, and existing and forthcoming agreements. Given this estimate the cashflows of the project should be adjusted. The adjustment is done by recalculating the cashflows assuming that the protection is reduced at a given date. The outcome is weighted by the probability that the said reduction will occur on the assumed date. The same process is repeated for other dates until all the distribution is "covered."

Second, given the identification and the evaluation of the vulnerability and the cost associated with this specific political contingency, management can try to reduce, or "manage," the political risk. In this case the question is what can the management offer to the government as an inducement to continue and maintain the current level of protection. In many countries, developing as well as developed, the government regards export as a national priority. (This was demonstrated in chapter 4 in the discussion of intra-industry trade.) By reorienting the project toward export, management can reduce the probability that the current protection will be eliminated or reduced. This is done in the original project presented above. The reduction, or the insurance of politicak risk, carries a price tag. The price is the difference, in present value terms, between the revised, small project and the large, export-oriented project.

It is outside the scope of this chapter to decide whether to insure the project against political risk by adopting the export version of the project or to opt for the high-risk, high-return version. (In reality management opted for the large, export-oriented project.) This example demonstrates that political risk can be and often is an important ingredient in the process of capital budgeting. It also demonstrates that management can manage political risk.

Notes

1. This chapter is partially based on a joint on-going research project with Stephen J. Kobrin.

6
Politics and Economics in the World's Financial Markets: An Uneasy Equilibrium

The Dynamics of Political Risk: Is the World Moving toward an International Financial Crisis?

Financial crises both domestic and international are not a modern phenomenon,[1] nor is the political content of such potential and realized crises. What is unique about the current concern with the potential for international financial crisis is its scope, its consequences, and the efforts being made to prevent its occurrence. In this regard international financial crises are like war: Wars are a permanent part of human nature and history, but modern wars affect more people and have more severe and lasting consequences than wars in the past, and therefore more efforts are devoted to the prevention of war. Indeed, a new world war may terminate the world as we know it. Such is the case with financial crisis. A new world financial crisis may affect the lives of more people than ever before. It may even terminate the world's financial and economic system as it exists today. Therefore, there are forces, political and economic alike, that act to negotiate differences in interests of various groups and countries in order to prevent an international financial crisis. Many of the solutions proposed, and almost all of those that are implemented, do satisfy both financial and political requirements. Because many of the reasons for the potential crisis are a combination of politics and economics, it is fitting, and necessary, to have political and economic solutions.

The main source for international financial crisis is the unwillingness, or the political inability, of various governments to accept the economic consequences of a given situation. In this respect the international monetary implicit crisis has a basis in fact. For example, one consequence of the change in the relative price in the world following the radical increase in the price of oil after 1973 was a worsening of the terms of trade of all oil importing countries. This effect was much more pronounced for the oil-importing LDCs.[2] One possible adjustment that could be made by the affected countries was to reduce consumption, both in the public and in the private sectors. This solution, which might be preferable from a point of view of market equilibrium, was not the politically preferred solution from the point of view of the LDCs. Therefore, they have attempted to maintain the then-current rate of consumption by borrowing. In terms of the economic model they have attempted to create an excess supply of bonds in exchange for their excess demand for goods. In other words, in order to be able to maintain the then-current consumption of oil in the new relative prices and to continue with the same level of consumption of other goods somebody had to buy their bonds. In a world where only economic, and therefore financial, considerations matter, the only way to create a demand for such infusion of new bonds is to convince the financial community that the return and the risk of these bonds make them a desirable financial asset. If somebody has to give up current consumption so that the governments and the citizens of at least some LDCs can increase theirs, this somebody should be compensated. Again, in purely economic terms this requires an increase in the marginal rate of return on investment in these LDCs. In this way, the additional return could be produced. This was not the case. First, the radical increase in the price of oil was associated with a world recession. This development in itself tends to lower profits, increase the demand for financing, and at the same time reduce the demand for capital assets. Second, the borrowed funds were not used primarily for investment. The purpose of the borrowing, given this simplified rendition, was to make more consumption possible. Thus the traditional self-liquidating project financing of earlier periods has been replaced by what is called balance-of-payments loans—loans against the general revenues of the borrowing countries. In order to induce supply of funds for this purpose, a higher effective rate of interest is required than would be the case without this process. The high rate of interest in real terms has a dampening effect on investment and economic activity, which in itself tends to create a downward pressure on the consumption level in many countries, including LDCs. If some of the affected countries are trying to continue and borrow to maintain earlier, and higher, consumption levels, as well as to service earlier debts at higher interest rates, a potential financial crisis is a likely possibility.[3] A close scrutiny of the process described above brings to mind two questions: The first one is why anybody would supply the funds to the borrowing LDCs if the purpose of the loan is known. The second question is how the world avoided the financial crisis although the borrowing process has been going strong for more than a decade. The answers to both of these questions are to be found in the interrelated areas of politics and economics.

The decision to borrow by the LDCs, or those LDCs who are capable of doing so, is a political decision. It is a political decision because it is carried out by a political organization. Also, at least some if not all of the reasons for borrowing are to be found at the political and social realms. Consumption-financing borrowing cannot be carried out by the private sector in the LDCs. Private-sector firms and individuals in those countries usually do not have access to the world's capital markets. Even if they do, they will not be able to support consumption-oriented loans. The will of the governments however, is a necessary but not sufficient condition. A sufficient condition is for a large country to support the political decisions of the governments of the involved LDCs. In this regard, the developed countries, and the U.S. government in particular, act as the implicit lender of the last resort. The U.S. government either by omission or by commission makes the transfer of real resources involved in the consumption-maintenance program possible. This process does not involve any particular risk and does not increase the potential of an international financial crisis if it is done in an explicit way: But this is not the case. Political reasons prevent an explicit mechanism for a transfer of resources to be implemented. Instead, various temporary arrangements are put into effect, usually when a problem arises. There are no hard and fast rules or explicit preannounced policy with regard to how much the LDCs can borrow in real term, what part of this is a subsidy, and who is paying the subsidy.[4]

The lack of clear policy decisions regarding the distributive effects of the international borrowing (and lending) creates the dynamics of political risk. Consider the following stylized facts. Given a change in the relative prices of a major commodity, or some other exogenous shock, an adjustment has to be made. The adjustment involves a redistribution of the world's income such that some groups or countries are better off and some are worse off. The adjustment that is consistent with the original change will lead to a stable equilibrium position. If, however, one group of countries is trying to avoid the consequences of the triggering change, this attempt creates disequilibrium. In order to sustain the disequilibrium (and by this turn it into an equilibrium situation, at least a transitory one), some other country or countries have to support the initial disequilibrium move. The support can be explicit or implicit. Both the initial move to avoid the original adjustment and the support given by the other country or countries are political by nature. The risk resides in the process by which political decisions are being made and implemented. The international monetary system is the conduit for the explicit and implicit decisions of the various actors. The potential for international financial crisis is the outcome of the dynamic process of actions and reactions by the various governments involved in the process. There are three basic ways of solving the problem: (1) revert to the economic solution, remove all governments' intervention, and let the market determine the necessary adjustments; (2) reach an explicit agreement of how the burden of the adjustment will be distributed (this solution requires some nonmarket institutional arrangement; these two solutions will reduce or even eliminate the political risk and with it the potential for international financial crisis); (3) do nothing explicit and try to accommodate the situation as need be (one cost of following this implicit solution is a high level of political risk and the resulting potential for financial crisis). In the last decade the third way out has been followed with regard to international lending to developing countries.

International Lending to Developing Countries: Is There an Inherent Collapse?

The lending to (and the borrowing by) developing countries in the financial markets of the world has become one of the central issues in international finance. What began as a rather small activity has grown to be a major process of international financial intermediation. The growth in the outstanding debt of the developing countries is documented in tables 6–1 and 6–2.

The data presented in tables 6–1 and 6–2 demonstrate three major characteristics of the LDCs debt: (1) the outstanding debt and therefore the debt service is growing; (2) most of the debt is located in a handful of countries (Mexico, Brazil, and Argentina account for a large proportion of the debt); (3) a major proportion of the outstanding debt is owed to commercial banks. Not only that, the outstanding debt is very large, both in absolute terms and compared to the debt capacity of the borrowing countries; it continues to grow even in the face of great awareness to the risk associated with the debt. In table 6–3 an estimate for the growth of the LDCs debt during the 1980s is presented.

The data presented in table 6–3 show clearly that the outstanding debt will grow. In 1984 and 1986 $40 to $50 billion of new money will be added to the outstanding debt. These sums are in addition to what is required to service the existing debt. In 1990, according to this estimate, the major twenty-one borrowers will borrow more than $350 billion. More than three-quarters of this amount will be needed to finance the then-existing debt. It appears that the process of international financial intermediation as well as the underlying process of a transfer of real resources from the developed to the developing countries is here to stay.

The issue of LDC debt has been the subject of much discussion in the recent years. Many studies have explored various aspects of the problem, and even the daily press devoted first-page stories to this issue.[5] Most of the economic literature is focusing on the demand for external finance by LDCs. For example, Kharas (1981), is employing a simple Harrod/Domar production model to derive the conditions under which the government of a given country will borrow externally to finance domestic expenditure plans. However,

Table 6–1
External Debt of LDCs, 1973–83
(billions of dollars)

	1973	1974	1975	1976	1977	1978	1979	1980	1981	1982	1983
Total outstanding debt	130.1	160.8	190.8	228.0	278.5	336.3	396.9	474.0	555.0	612.4	664.3
Short-term debt	18.4	22.7	27.3	33.2	42.5	49.7	58.8	85.5	102.2	112.7	92.4
Long-term debt	111.8	138.1	163.5	194.9	235.9	286.6	338.1	388.5	452.8	499.6	571.6
By type of creditor:											
Official creditors	51.0	60.1	70.3	82.4	98.7	117.5	133.0	152.9	172.4	193.2	218.7
Government	37.3	43.4	50.3	57.9	67.6	79.1	87.2	98.7	108.6	120.4	135.3
International institutions	13.7	16.6	20.0	24.8	31.0	38.4	45.8	54.2	63.8	72.8	83.3
Private creditors	60.8	77.9	95.1	114.8	137.3	169.1	205.1	235.6	280.4	306.4	353.0
Unguaranteed debt	29.3	36.0	40.8	45.9	51.4	56.4	67.3	77.5	96.7	103.9	113.7
Guaranteed debt	31.5	52.4	52.4	66.6	85.9	112.7	137.8	158.1	183.7	202.2	239.3
Financial institutions	17.3	36.7	36.7	49.0	59.1	79.5	102.9	121.6	144.5	159.5	193.8
Other private creditors	14.2	17.6	17.6	19.8	26.8	33.2	34.9	36.5	39.2	42.7	45.5
Debt service payments	17.9	25.1	25.1	27.8	34.7	50.3	65.0	76.2	94.7	107.1	93.2
Interest	6.9	10.5	10.5	10.9	13.6	19.4	28.0	40.4	55.1	59.2	55.1
Amortization	11.1	14.6	14.6	16.8	21.1	30.9	36.9	35.8	39.7	47.9	38.1
External debt/exports	115.4	122.4	122.4	125.5	126.4	130.2	119.2	112.9	124.9	143.3	144.4
External debt/GNP	22.4	21.8	23.8	25.7	27.4	28.5	27.5	27.6	31.0	34.7	34.7

Source: *World Economic Outlook* (1983). Reported in Barth and Pelzman (1984).

Table 6–2
Bank Claims on the Major Borrower, 1975–82[a]
(billion of U.S. dollars)

	(a) Claims on All Countries	(b) Claims on Argentina, Brazil, and Mexico	(b) as a Percentage of (a)
1975	62.7	31.5	50.24
1976	80.9	42.5	52.53
1977	94.3	50.2	53.23
1978	131.3	63.2	48.13
1979	171.0	83.0	48.53
1980	210.2	108.1	51.42
1981	253.5	134.5	53.06
1982[a]	268.3	145.0	54.04

Source: Barth and Pelzman (1984).
[a] June data.

Table 6–3
An Estimate of the Development of LDCs' Debt, 1984–90[a]
(billions of dollars)

	1981	1984	1986	1990
Major 21 borrowers				
Gross borrowing	215.9	195.1	241.2	354.3
Amortization	38.2	31.3	49.5	88.7
Short-term rollover	97.9	123.2	124.4	183.7
New money	79.7	40.8	49.3	81.9
Argentina				
Gross borrowing	22.3	13.0	15.9	16.1
Amortization	3.5	2.7	5.3	6.5
Short-term rollover	10.3	8.3	8.7	9.6
New money	8.5	2.5	1.9	0
Brazil				
Gross borrowing	30.7	20.3	28.8	37.7
Amortization	7.5	1.6	11.6	17.8
Short-term rollover	12.9	10.5	11.8	15.9
New money	10.3	8.2	5.4	4.0
Mexico				
Gross borrowing	45.5	30.0	34.7	53.6
Amortization	6.4	3.5	11.5	28.6
Short-term rollover	12.7	22.8	19.9	18.6
New money	26.4	3.7	3.3	6.4

Source: *World Financial Markets* (February 1984).
[a] Data for 1984, 1986, and 1990 are estimates.

by employing the Harrod/Domar production framework, it is assumed that the funds are used for investment purposes. Like many other simplified macroeconomic models of this kind, there is no specification for a government utility function, or some other model of government behavior, as a political and economic actor. A more flexible approach allows for savings behavior to affect the development and growth of the debt. When consumption is added to the picture, it can be shown that given net capital inflows consumption can exceed domestic income. In such a case, discussed by Takagi (1981), debt problems are associated with consumption rather than with inefficient investment. More specifically, some of the consumption-based debt-problem models are based on the assumption that at least public consumption is a function of net capital inflows. This approach is consistent with the balance-of-payments loans discussed earlier in this chapter. Another type of economic-based debt-management model are growth-optimization models with external financing. Like the Harrod/Domar models the motivation for the borrowing is a process that equalizes the cost of financing to the intertemporal marginal productivity of capital. It should be noted that such models (e.g., Hamada 1969) lead to very high levels of borrowing if the true cost of finance intemporally is zero or close to zero for the borrowing agency. This will also justify consumption (noninvestment) uses of the borrowed funds. Other researchers have introduced consumption smoothing as a rational for the financing of investment by external borrowing. This issue is closely related to the issue of postponing or avoiding what would be necessary adjustments in the absence of external finance. Agmon, Lessard, and Paddock (1979) have analyzed the optimal adjustment pattern following the change in the relative prices of oil. However, in order to derive the optimal demand for loans by LDCs, one has to know the supply conditions. Supply conditions depend on the desire and ability of ultimate suppliers of funds to transfer the resources necessary to the financial institutions that actually make the transfer possible.

Put in other words, the issue of the international borrowing of (lending to) LDCs in the financial markets of the world can be presented from three different perspectives. The heart of the matter is a process of a transfer of real resources from a group of developed countries to a group of developing countries. This real transfer is associated with monetary changes that affect the real transfer and cause many other side effects, such as an increase in the level of risk in the world market. The actual transfer, or most of it, is carried for the last decade by the international commercial banking system. The well-publicized crisis in LDC debt may refer to a cessation of the transfer in the affected countries. An attempt to alleviate the debt situation by a large-scale monetization of the debt and the debt service may create a new wave of inflation. This may be regarded as a monetary crisis. A failure of the financial intermediation system, and a resulting change in the way by which the real transfer is affected, is a third type of possible crisis. Although the most talked about crisis is a banking crisis—that is, a failure of the international financial intermediation system—this is not necessarily the riskiest facet of the current situation.

As it is amply demonstrated by McDonald (1982), the literature is limited on the supply conditions, which are crucial in the understanding of the probability and the nature of a possible crisis. Kindleberger (1978) has attempted to describe and analyze the phenomenon of a financial intermediation crisis from a historical perspective. But his illuminating presentation leaves many questions unanswered. A more quantitative approach is followed by a recent study by Feder and Ross (1982). Their estimates lead to the conclusion that the expected loss as it is expressed by the market rates of interest is quite low. This approach is consistent with a view that downgrades the probability of a banking crisis as a result of an avalanche of unperforming loans.[6] Another view is presented by credit-rationing models. Credit rationing (as presented for example by Sachs 1981 and Sachs and Cohen 1982) may imply a crisis of the first type because it may limit the real transfer. Obviously, the three types of potential crises are related. A limit on credit in gross borrowing terms may lead to a real transfer from the LDCs to the developing countries. This may force default. The default may bring about an attempt to rescue the banking system by a large-scale monetization, which may create a crisis due to an unanticipated increase in the rate of inflation. Such an increase will lead to a surge in nominal interest rates, which in itself will affect both the process of real transfer and the stability of the financial intermediation system.

The LDCs borrowers have an interest in preventing what to them may be a crisis in the real transfer. They would regard a change in the direction of the transfer, or even a cessation of the net transfer, as a crisis situation. The industrialized countries have an interest in preventing a financial intermediation crisis—that is, a failure of the banking system and a monetary crisis. The banking system affects every facet of modern life. This is more pronounced in highly developed countries like the United States, Japan, the United Kingdom, and the countries of Western Europe. A failure of one function of the banking system (international lending and borrowing) may bring about total collapse. The economic and political cost of such a development is very high. A surge in the inflation, due to large-scale monetization of external debts of LDCs, also carry a high economic and political price tag. The political successes of the Reagan administration in the United States and of the Thatcher government in the United Kingdom in the early 1980s constitute an evidence for the assertion that high inflation has become untenable politically. Therefore, a community of interest supports and maintains the current situation. The current situation is characterized by a continuation of the net trans-

Table 6–4
Rescheduling Packages and Debt Capacity Indicators, mid-1983

Country	Amount of Package (B$)	Debt as Percentage of GNP	Debt Percentage of Exports
Argentina	1.75	53	424
Brazil	4.40	43	359
Chile	1.30	90	290
Mexico	5.10	61	275
Peru	0.45	65	331
Nigeria	1.60	NA	NA

Source: *World Financial Markets* (September 1983).

fer to at least some LDCs. (This is demonstrated by forecasted injections of new money through 1990 in table 6–3.) It is also characterized by negotiated solutions to the banking problems. This custom-made approach is evident by a relatively large number of rescheduling packages. The reschedulings are localized solutions that have little effect on the world rate of inflation compared to a large-scale monetization. Data on some recent rescheduling packages are presented in table 6–4.

The debt capacity indicators suggest that the rescheduling is done to maintain the system rather than to affect a future repayment of the debt.[7] Yet this policy (more implicit than explicit) of maintaining the above-mentioned community of interests by providing case-by-case temporary solutions seems to be working. One consequence of this policy is an increase in the political risk in the world. Interaction of the political and economic factors and the resulting increase in the level of the risk, are presented in a model in the following section.

International Taxation and International Lending: An Explanatory Model of Political Economy[8]

In the first two sections of this chapter it was asserted that the center of what is known as the crisis of international borrowing by (lending to) LDCs is a process of a transfer of real resources from at least some developed countries to a group of LDCs. It has been suggested also that the motivation for this transfer is at least as political as it is economic. In this section the assertion and its corrolary are buffeted by a positive, empirical observation and by a normative explanatory model.

Some of the banking literature has adopted commercial banking lending procedures to evaluate the creditworthiness of various LDCs.[9] By most standards employed by loan officers in the process of credit granting, most if not all of the heavy borrowers among the LDCs do not qualify. In a recent study Agmon and Dietrich (1983) went beyond the level of casual empiricism employed in earlier studies. The explanatory power of the common measures of credit measure was tested with regard to the growth of outstanding debt by LDCs. Measures for creditworthiness were computed for the LDCs for which data was available in the OECD publication *Geographical Distribution of Financial Flows to Developing Countries*. The rates of growth in the GNP (GROGNP) were computed for all the countries for the periods 1977 to 1978 and 1978 to 1979. The ratio of outstanding debt to international reserves (RESRAT) was taken as a measure of liquidity. The ability to support the loan was estimated by the ratio of the country's balance of payments (current account surplus) to net borrowing (BOPRAT). Another measure was computed by taking the ratio of scheduled debt service to the GNP (SUCRAT). The growth of private lending, except of trade-related financing, was regressed on the four dependent variables for the two periods on a cross-sectional basis. A similar regression was estimated for a pooled time-series and cross-sectional sample. The results are presented in table 6–5.

None of the traditional measures for creditworthiness had any explanatory power. Three of the four variables in the pooled sample have the wrong sign, although all of them are not much different than zero. The only variable that has some explanatory power is the debt-service ratio. However, contrary to normal credit-granting procedures, it is positively related to the rate of growth of the debt. (The rate of growth is expressed relative to the GNP of the country in question.) Further statistical analysis done by Agmon and Dietrich supports the hypothesis that the rate of growth of the debt can be explained by the need to service the debt without reducing other public or private expenditures. The estimates for the future rate of growth of the debt presented in table 6–3 are based on this proposition as well.

If traditional credit analysis as applied to LDC borrowing (and to banks' lending to them) fails to provide an explanation to this major international financial phenomenon, what can? The following is an alternative explanation.[10] The basic assumption of the model is that the financial activities, lending and borrowing, are employed as a convenient way to affect a redistribution of income in the world.

The participants in the process of income redistribution are governments and financial institutions. Governments are assumed to be active players who have objective functions of their own. This utility function may or may not represent the community over which they have jurisdiction. Financial institutions are firms that operate in order to maximize their market value given

Table 6–5
The Explanatory Power of Traditional Credit Measure for LDCs, 1978–79

	1978 Cross-Section		1979 Cross-Section		1978–79 Pooled Sample	
	Coefficient Estimate	*t-test*	*Coefficient Estimate*	*t-test*	*Coefficient Estimate*	*t-test*
Intercept	−0.0095	−0.75	0.0190	1.82	0.0121	1.51
RESRAT	−0.0040	−1.41	0.0013	0.68	−7.363E-05	−0.04
BOPRAT	−0.0066	−1.21	0.0045	0.69	−0.0014	−0.32
GROGNP	0.0732	1.74	0.0015	0.07	0.0091	0.48
SUCRAT	1.4602	3.06	0.1274	0.41	0.4977	1.81
F	2.86	—	0.54	—	1.36	—
R^2	0.45	—	0.13	—	0.14	—

Source: Agmon and Dietrich (1983).

market conditions. These conditions include government policies whether they are explicit or implicit. Income distribution among countries is jointly determined by political and economic factors.

Public-sector expenditure is assumed to reflect the decision of the government as an institution, and at least to some extent it serves the self-interest of the government (e.g., to be reelected). Therefore the distribution of income derived from the pure economic process of exchange (given production) is often adjusted to reflect the distribution of political power.

Each government has the power to act within its jurisdiction. This power can give rise to credible threats to harm others by unilateral action. The threats may be explicit or implicit. The political power also gives some governments the ability to transfer income from one national unit to another. These international transfers can be carried out either directly by taxes and subsidies or indirectly by changing relative prices through tariffs and other indirect taxes.

Assume a world with N principals where the governments are the principals. The banks act as agents for the principals. Each one of the principals (a government) has a certain endowment (the country's wealth). The aggregate endowment of all the principals is the total wealth in the world. This wealth can be redistributed in a way that is different than the original distribution of the endowments. Each one of the principals derives income. (The issue of how the income is distributed among the residents of a given principal is ignored here.) The income of a given principal can be defined as

$$I_j = r_j W_j + T_j, j = 1, 2, \ldots, N \text{ principals (countries)} \quad (6.1)$$

where I_j = income of country j

W_j = endowment of country j

r_j = rate of return on endowment at country j

T_j = transfer payment of country j

T_j can be negative, positive or zero. We assume that r_j and W_j are constants for any country j. The only variable that can affect income is T_j the transfer of payment. We assume that each and every country (principal) would like to maximize its total I_j. Given the constraint of total wealth in the world $\sum_{j=1}^{N} T_j = 0$. Therefore two general solutions are possible. Either $T_j = 0$ for all j, or for some countries T is positive and for some it is negative. In the first case there are no transfer payments in the world. This situation renders the model irrelevant. Also it does not appear to provide an explanation for the observed phenomenon. Therefore the discussion is focused on all other cases where for some j, $T_j \neq 0$. In this case the countries of the world can be divided into two subsets. The first subset consists of the transfer payers, and the second of the receivers of the transfer. Let the members of the first subset be denoted by k, $k = 1,2, \ldots , K$, and the second by subscript e, $e = K + 1, K + 2, \ldots , N$. It follows that $T_k < 0$, $T_e > 0$ and

$$\sum_{K=1}^{K} T_k + \sum_{e=K+1}^{N} T_e = 0 \qquad (6.2)$$

The question now is, What is the motivation of any country to be in a situation where it is a part of the first group, where $T_k < 0$? The answer has to do with the ability of the countries that belong to the second subset (transfer recipients) to pose a credible threat. In his classic treatment of the subject, Schelling (1960) defines a threat as ". . . that one asserts that he will do in a contingency, what he manifestly prefers not to do if the contingency will not occur, the contingency being governed by the second party's behavior. . . ."[11] Threats can be explicit or implicit, specific or general. In general the aim of the threatening party is to change the behavior of the threatened party.

In this case the purpose of the threats is to generate transfer payments. For example, suppose that country e_1 is located next to country K_1. Assume further that country e_1 is small relative to country K_1. The government of country e_1 approaches the government of K_1 asking for a transfer payment. If the transfer is refused, the current government of e_1 threatens to resign. In this highly simplified case, if there is a probability that the next government of e_1 will be hostile to K_1, the government of K_1 will be ready to pay the government of e_1 to avoid the possible realization of the threat. The maximum payment that the government of K_1 will be ready to pay is

$$^{T}K_1 e_1 = PD \qquad (6.3)$$

where $^{T}K_1 e_1$ is the transfer payment from K_1 to e_1. P is the joint probability that the government of e_1 will resign and that it will be replaced by a government hostile to K_1. D is the additional net defense expenditures given that an adverse change in the government of e_1 takes place.

In this analysis, D is that part of the gross defense expenditure that is considered waste. That is, D does not contribute to the welfare of the community except that it balances the adverse change in the environment. The value of P depends on the credibility of the threat of the government of e_1 to resign. Another way to look at P is as the probability that in the absence of the transfer payment the government of e_1 will be forced out of power.[12]

Because *P* contains many subjective components the actual "solution" always involves negotiation.

Actual threats might not be as extreme as the example described above. Some threats may be more implicit. Others may be directed at the agents of the principals—that is, at the banks rather than at the government. The situation of Argentina is a case in point. By threatening a default on its bank loans, Argentina was able to effect a transfer payment from the U.S. government. However, in this case both the transfer and the threat were implicit.

The ability to generate transfer payment does not reside exclusively in the ability to pose a credible threat. The notion that some countries deserve "special considerations" in terms of income redistribution is not new, nor is it limited to the LDCs of today. Rimmer (1979) developed a concept of the have-not status. The have-not status is ". . . the condition of a country that is disadvantaged economically in the world community and to which international concessions are therefore due. . . ."[13] Rimmer shows that Germany, Japan, and Italy demanded and received have-not status in the period between World War I and World War II. Their assumed disadvantage was not having colonies. It is obvious that the concessions given to these countries reflect a distribution of political power (including the ability to pose a credible threat) more than a pure economic process of exchange and production.

The process of income redistribution in the world through transfer mechanism can be viewed as a world tax. The tax is levied by the have-not countries. The ability to tax varies from one country to another and reflects both needs and power to have the needs attended to. In principle, the world-tax system could operate on a direct government-to-government basis. In reality, this process of real transfer is aided both by the monetary process and by the process of international financial intermediation by the banking system.

Borrowing in the financial worlds of the market can be viewed as deferred taxes or as a permanent increase in both current and future "taxes" that the developed countries, and most of all the United States, are transfering to some developing countries. These LDCs are borrowing today from the banks against future tax revenues. This is similar to the case where the U.S. Treasury borrows money by selling Treasury bills against future and current tax receipts of the U.S. government. In both cases, the domestic and the international, the real case is not solvency but liquidity. As long as the debt is serviced, repayment is not a real problem because the debt can and should be viewed as permanent.

The difference between the domestic and the international situation is in the ability of the U.S. government (or any government in its domestic market) to tax its own residents compared to the ability of the government of the major LDCs borrowers to effect the necessary transfer payment. Hence, the political risk.

Is the Political Risk Located in Mexico City or in Washington, D.C.?

In the beginning of this chapter it was argued that the potential for financial crisis in the financial markets of the world has political roots. The model presented in the last section suggests that the political risk is located with the transferring country rather than with the borrowing country. If this is so, then the current country-risk analysis that focuses on the major LDC borrowers is misplaced. Teams of researchers should descend on Washington, D.C., rather than on Mexico City or Buenos Aires.

The issue of the location of the political risk has important implications for the cost associated with this risk. The vehicle used to transfer the risk has important implications for how the inherent political risk is allocated among various participants in the markets of the world.

One of the stepping stones of modern financial economics is the concept of diversification and systematic risk.[14] The basic features of these twin concepts are that all financial assets are held in a well-diversified portfolio. This portfolio may include a very large number of various securities denominated in many currencies and reflecting real economic activities in many countries around the world.[15] The risk of any particular activity, which is measured by the volatility of the return on a given financial asset, depends most on the covariance between the changes in the price (volatility) of the said asset and the changes in the price of an index that represents the portfolio. Following this line of argument the cost of the risk, or the required risk premium, depends to a large extent on the location of the political risk. The location of the risk affects the covariance between the political risk component of a given financial asset and the relevant market portfolio. To understand this point, consider the following example. Suppose that the relevant portfolio is the world portfolio: that is, financial decisions are made at the margin by large institutional investors that hold highly diversified portfolios including different financial assets (CDs, bonds, stocks, and other specialized securities) denominated in a number of currencies. Risk is measured relative to this portfolio. In other words, in order to evaluate the change in the value of a given loan (the loan is viewed as a financial asset), the potential change is measured by evaluating the contribution of the change of the value of the loan to a change in the value of a multisecurity portfolio. This change is measured basically by the covariance, which in itself is determined by the correlation between the future changes in the value of the loan and the future average changes in the value of the portfolio. If the change in the market value of the loan as a financial asset (that is, the probability of arrears, partial default, or total default) depends on the political actions of small and isolated countries, then the correlation should be very low or even zero. This is so because there is no relationship between the process that governs the changes in the return on the market portfolio and the isolated political actions of small individual countries that do not act in concert. On the other hand, if the market value of the loan depends on the political action of a government of a major country, then the correlation coefficient, as well as the systematic risk, is likely to be very high. This is so because a failure by the U.S. government to support the debt of the major LDCs borrower in a way suggested in the last section above will have repercussions for all securities' markets. Therefore, it will have a greater effect on the world portfolio and therefore on the level of the systematic risk associated with the debt situation.

It may sound paradoxical, but the "classic" approach to political risk that places the emphasis on radical and "irresponsible" policies of LDCs leads to a conclusion that political risk is almost totally unsystematic. Therefore it does not matter. What may appear as a less radical approach that locates the political risk in the United States and other Western industrialized countries actually makes political risk more risky. When the source of political risk is the legislative and regulatory actions of major governments rather than violent and unpredictable changes in small and isolated countries, political risk becomes systematic: It becomes an integral part of the major financial markets of the world. Therefore it does matter and should be studied and integrated into the mainstream of modern financial theory.

It follows that the evergrowing outstanding debt of some LDCs is risky, not because Argentina or Mexico or Brazil may default on its loan. As has been demonstrated earlier, these countries do not possess the capability and the willingness to repay the debt. The debt is risky because political pressures within the United States may prevent the U.S. government from providing the implicit guarantees and the explicit real transfers that are necessary in order to continue, support, and service, the outstanding debt.

The second and related issue is who bears the risk associated with the debt and whether the current arrangement whereby the risk is intermediated and allocated by the banking system is an efficient solution.

The question of the allocation of the risk between the LDCs borrowers (the "south") and the Western industrialized lenders (the "north") has not been a subject of much research. One common argument is that the banks have created an inefficient allocation of the risk associated with the international lending to (borrowing of) LDCs. This is so because the banks have made a large number of risky loans to LDCs with a typical maturity of five to seven years. At the same time, the banks have mobilized funds from investors in the world in the form of short-term and nominally riskless deposits. Some of the researchers in the field of international north/south transfers argue that this policy contributes to an increase in the level of the risk of the international lending. Diaz Alejandro (1984) argues that the situation in the financial markets can be summarized by the phrase: "Imperfection markets and clever agents," whereby the banks are the "clever agents" who took advantage of the imperfection and filled the gap for a fee. Lessard (1983) points out that the numeraire (which is dollars deflated by the change in the interest rates) is negatively correlated with the income of most LDCs. This is so because an increase in the nominal rate of interest increases the debt service and therefore the total outstanding debt of the major LDC borrowers. At the same time an increase in the interest rates in dollar terms have a dampening effect on the exports revenues of these countries. It follows that if the debt repayment ability resides in the borrower countries, a numeraire that is positively related to exports revenues is needed. Lessard points out some existing and potential arrangements of this kind. This approach is rooted in the assumption that the income to service and maybe to repay the debt should be generated within the borrowing countries. Given this assumption, the current arrangement is inefficient in terms of risk-shifting and risk-allocation.

If, on the other hand, an approach is taken that is similar to the one presented by Agmon and Dietrich (1983), the inefficiency is more apparent than real. To demonstrate this point consider the following problem: Assume that the government of the United States decides to transfer a certain amount of real resources to Mexico. For a variety of political and organizational reasons the U.S. government does not wish to carry out the transfer by a direct government-to-government grant or by a concessional loan. Rather than doing that, the U.S. government establishes a credit line with a commercial bank and instructs the bank to lend the funds to the Mexican government or to its agencies. Assume that the loan has a maturity of seven years. On the balance sheet of the bank, the loan is listed as a long-term (seven-year) asset. The management of the bank knows, however, that this loan represents a permanent line of credit with the U.S. government. This line is basically a series of short-term loans that are riskless in terms of U.S. dollars. As a result the bank matches the Mexican debt by a series of roll-over short-term U.S. dollars deposits. On the balance sheet it looks like the bank has a serious mismatch between assets and liabilities. It has a long-term risky asset, a loan to Mexico, and short-term riskless assets, Eurodollar three-month deposits. Given the view expressed above, there is no mismatch. The bank has a good match both in maturity and in risk.

The answer to the question of whether the current arrangement (where the real transfer is affected by a process of financial intermediation) is efficient as a mechanism to allocate risk depends on where the risk is located. If the risk is located in Mexico City and Buenos Aires, then the current arrangement adds financial risk to the already existing country risk. If, on the other hand, the political risk is located in Washington, D.C., then the current financing of the LDCs debt by the commercial banks is a risk-efficient arrangement.

Notes

1. For a history and an analysis of financial crises, see Kindleberger (1978).
2. For a more formal and complete analysis of the effects of the change in the price of oil on the terms of trade of LDCs, see Agmon and Laffer (1978).
3. The process of the development of a financial crisis both in the U.S. and the world's market is the subject of a number of studies by Minsky. For a recent analysis, see Minsky (1984).
4. This subject is discussed further in "International Taxation and International Lending" below.
5. A detailed survey and analysis of the economic literature on LDCs debt is presented by McDonald (1982). For a typical newspaper treatment of this subject, see "Latin Nations, Creditors Near Confrontation," *Los Angeles Times,* April 15, 1984.
6. This approach is also consistent with the politically motivated model presented by Agmon and Dietrich (1983).
7. This is also suggested by the continuing rescheduling through 1983 and 1984. For example, another $500 million package was negotiated by Argentina in spring 1984. In most cases the rescheduling package was not effectively related to a long-term reduction in either public-sector or private-sector consumption in the receiving countries.
8. This section is partly adapted from Agmon and Dietrich (1983).
9. For example, see Saini and Bates (1978), Sargen (1977), and Weintraub (1983).
10. The model was originally discussed in Agmon and Dietrich (1983):sec. 2.
11. Schelling (1960):123.
12. This has happened in a number of countries in Latin America and elsewhere.
13. Rimmer (1979):307.
14. These concepts are now the bread and butter of modern finance. For an excellent description, see Brealey and Myers (1984):chs. 7–8.
15. For an analysis of international investment activities within the paradigm of modern financial economics, see Agmon and Lessard (1977).

References

Agmon, T., and J. Kimbal Dietrich. 1983. "International Lending and Income Redistribution: An Alternative View of Country Risk." *Journal of Banking and Finance* (December):483–96.

Agmon, T., and D.R. Lessard. 1977. "Investor Recognition of Corporate International Diversification." *Journal of Finance* (September):1049–55.

Agmon, T., D.R. Lessard, and J.L. Paddock. 1979. "Financial Markets and the

Adjustment to Higher Oil Prices." In *Advances in the Economics of Energy and Resources,* vol. 1, edited by R. Pindyck. (JAI Press).

Barth, J.R., and J. Pelzman. 1984. "International Debt: Conflict and Resolution." Department of Economics, George Mason University, Fairfax, Va.

Brealey, R., and S. Myers. 1984. *Principles of Corporate Finance,* 2d ed. (New York: McGraw-Hill).

Diaz-Alejandro, C.F. 1984. "Some Financial Issues in the North, in the South, and in Between." In *The Future of the International Monetary System,* edited by T. Agmon, R.G. Hawkins, and R.M. Levich. (Lexington, Mass.: Lexington Books).

Feder, G., and K. Ross. 1982. "Risk Assessments and Risk Premiums in the Euro-dollar Market." *Journal of Finance* (June):679–91.

Geographical Distribution of Financial Flows to Developing Countries. Organization for Economic Cooperation and Development 1978, 1979.

Hamada, K. 1969. "Optimal Capital Accumulation by an Economy Facing an International Capital Market, pt. 2." *Journal of Political Economy* (July/August): 684–97.

Kharas, H. 1981. "The Analysis of Long-Run Creditworthiness: Theory and Practice." World Bank Domestic Finance Study No. 73. (July) Washington, D.C.

Kindleberger, C.P. 1978. *Manias, Panics, and Crashes: A History of Financial Crisis* (New York: Basic Books).

"Latin Nations, Creditors Near Confrontation." *Los Angeles Times* April 15, 1984.

Lessard, D.R. 1983. "North–South: The Implications for Multinational Banking." *Journal of Banking and Finance* (December):521–32.

McDonald, D.C. 1982. "Debt Capacity and Developing Country Borrowing: A Survey of the Literature." *IMF Staff Papers* 603–46.

Minsky, H.P. 1984. "The Potential for Financial Crisis." In *The Future of the International Monetary System,* edited by T. Agmon, R.G. Hawkins, and R.M. Levich. (Lexington, Mass.: Lexington Books).

Rimmer, G. 1979. "The Have and the Have-not." In *Economic Development and Cultural Change* (Chicago, Ill.: University of Chicago).

Sachs, J.D. 1981. "The Current Account and Macroeconomic Adjustment in the 1970s." *Brookings Papers on Economic Activity* 1:201–68.

Sachs, J.D., and D. Cohen. 1982. "LDC Borrowing with Default Risk." NBER Working Paper 925 (July).

Saini, K., and P. Bates. 1978. "Statistical Techniques for Determining Debt-Capacity for Developing Countries: Analytical Review of the Literature and Further Empirical Results." Federal Reserve Bank of New York Research Paper 7818 (September).

Sargen, N. 1977. "Economic Indicators and Country Risk Appraisal." Federal Reserve Bank of San Francisco *Economic Review* (Fall):19–35.

Schelling, T. 1960. *Theory of Conflicts* (Cambridge, Mass.: Harvard University Press).

Takagi, 1981. "Aid and Debt Problems in Less Developed Countries." *Oxford Economic Papers,* New Series, vol. 33 (July):323–37.

Weintraub, R.E. 1983. "International Debt: Crisis and Challenge." Department of Economics, George Mason University, Fairfax, Va.

7
Conclusions

Political Risk is Here to Stay

A major premise of this book is that political risk is an integral part of the economic activity in the markets of the world. Economic activity does not take place in a vacuum, nor is it divorced from other forms of human activities. Politics may benefit a certain firm or a certain investment or a financial transaction. In other times or for other transactions political factors may be costly. In both of these cases, politics is an important input for decision. (The terms *politics* and *political factors* are used here in the broad sense that was defined in chapter one.)

The fact that business decisions are made within a political context is not new and does not require special analytic tools. All business decisions are made on the basis of all pertinent information, including political information. This book has emphasized the uncertain nature of political decisions and their impact on financial and investment decisions of the firm.

Governments and other political organizations are becoming more powerful. This reflects the implicit preferences of most people; they vote for political parties that practice intervention even if they preach free market. It also reflects a more complex world with many conflicting views and goals. In this case the well-known saying on the nature of democracy may be valid: The current political process is chaotic and uncertain, but it may be the best arrangement.

Given this view, the uncertainty in the world—which is the outcome of the political process described in the preceding chapters—is a permanent fixture. Political risk is here to stay, and financial and investment decisions have to take this type of risk into account.

The actual behavior of firms and individual investors in the markets of the world supports this view. Political-risk shelters such as external currency markets, intracompany transactions, and other vehicles of avoidance, as well as negotiating devices, are all testimony that the market has realized the cost of political risk and done something about it.

For example, since the beginning of the 1970s, the attitude toward the nature of the exchange-rate system has undergone continuous development. In the period 1971 to 1973 the pegged exchange-rate system, known as the Bretton Woods system, was replaced by a hybrid of a floating exchange-rate system that allowed a certain level of intervention and currency areas that maintained a limited version of the pegged system. The new system was introduced as a temporary arrangement and as an accommodating measure to solve political problems for some countries. At that time the U.S. dollar was very weak compared to the major European currencies and the Japanese yen. More than ten years passed, and the U.S. dollar became once again the strongest currency in the world. Those countries that intervened in the past because their currency was too strong are intervening now because their currency is too weak. Then and now, the intervention is used to accommodate political needs. As such it increases the uncertainty in the exchange market. Yet in the last ten years or so, the system took hold of the market because the exchange-rate system now in operation reflects the political uncertainty in the determination of the exchange rates.

The market has realized both the nature of the current system and what it stands for, as well as the very small real chance for a change to a more stable system. To this day most of the business writers and spokesmen prefer a return to a fixed or a pegged exchange-rate system. They also realize that the current system is a mirror to the political risk in the market. The exchange-rate system can be replaced when the political conditions in the world change. The political risk itself is a direct outcome of the political system in which we all live. Because this system is not about to change, neither is the exchange-rate system.

On the basis of this implicit understanding, business firms and individuals develop financial instruments and procedures to cope with the political risk expressed by the exchange-rate system. The currency options markets and interest rates and currency swaps transactions are two major responses of the market to this new and riskier environment. The response is evidence that the market has realized that political risk is, and will remain, a major component of the economic and financial environment.

The Political Economy of International Finance: Positive Explanations and Normative Implications

The main thrust of this study has been that political risk is a pervasive part of almost all financial and investment decisions. As such it affects much of the activity in the financial markets of the world. The understanding and the recognition of the role of political risk in the financial markets and in corporate finance has positive and normative implications.

On the positive side understanding and recognizing political risk contribute to a better understanding of many developments in the markets and within firms. The existence of external currency markets side by side with the controlled domestic money market is one major example. The sharp changes in relative prices—both as a result of independent changes as in the case of oil prices and as an outcome of changes in the rate of inflation—is another. The so-called crisis situation in the international banking community associated with the lending to developing countries is another case that can be better understood when political factors are taken into account. In this case the analysis shows that quite a bit of risk exists in the markets as a result of this lending but that the risk is political in nature.

Integrating political considerations into corporate finance is particularly appropriate in the case of the multinational corporation. The development of this business organization is a response to imperfect market conditions and to barriers to free movement of factors of production, goods, and services. Many of the existing barriers are better understood in political terms. This is particularly true in the field of international trade, where whole industries operate and investment decisions are being made on the basis of import substitution and other politically motivated arguments.

Positive explanations are of more interest to the researcher and the observer than to the investor or the practicing manager. Investors and managers are interested in what can be done and what should be done from now on. Two major normative implications emerge from the argument developed and presented in this study: (1) Political considerations and the resulting political risk have to be explicitly recognized in investment decisions; (2) once they have been recognized and quantified, a number of methods may be implemented to reduce or to otherwise manage this type of risk.

An explicit recognition of political risk as an integral part of financial management will undoubtedly spur the development of techniques to measure and handle political risk. In this way recognition and understanding will contribute to the normative aspect of management.

Index

About the Author

Tamir Agmon is associate professor of international finance on the faculty of management at Tel Aviv University and a visiting professor for international business at the graduate school of business administration at the University of Southern California at Los Angeles. Professor Agmon has written many articles in scholarly journals and has edited two books, *Multinational Corporations from Small Countries* (MIT Press, 1977) and *The Future of the International Monetary System* (Lexington Books, 1984).

Professor Agmon has extensive experience in consulting in international finance, international banking, and corporate finance. He is working as a consultant in Israel, the United States, and the Far East; his clients include banks such as Bank Leumi and Chase Manhattan Bank, large corporations such as Mitsui, Koor Industries, PACECO, and the Israel Electric Corporation, and government agencies such as the Economic Development Board in Singapore. Professor Agmon is a member of the board of directors of two Israeli companies.